D0514155

AM I NORMAL?

Anita Naik lives in London, where she was born and brought up. She never dreamed she'd land her ideal job of writing for *Just Seventeen*, but now finds herself the magazine's hugely popular agony aunt, advising thousands of teenage girls on their problems. Anita also regularly writes features for *Smash Hits*, *19* and *FHM* magazines. As if this isn't enough to keep her busy, Anita is currently studying for a counselling and psychotherapy course and also does voluntary work for human rights charity Survival International. On rare days off, Anita enjoys sitting in cafés, people-watching. Previous books include *Coping With Crushes*, *Single Again*, and the *Just Seventeen Quiz Book*.

AM I NORMAL?

by ANITA NAIK

illustrations by James Tyrrell

Hodder
Children's
Books

FOR MY PARENTS

'**I**f you compare yourself with others, you may become vain and bitter. For always there will be greater and lesser persons than yourself.'

Desiderata

Introduction

Imagine a world where we all looked the same, had the same hair colour and grew to the same height. Where we could guarantee we would hit puberty at 13 years old, get a boyfriend at 16 years old, have two parents who loved each other forever. A world where we would know exactly the right thing to say at exactly the right moment. A world where we would never get embarrassed, never have doubts about ourselves and never have to worry about spots or body hair. Ridiculous? Of course it is, but this is what many of us imagine the world is like for 'normal' people. And thousands of us worry we aren't a part of it.

But if there's one true thing in life, it's that there is no such thing as 'normal'. Our bodies are all different, our lives are often odd and at times we all feel that no one understands us. But in fact it's exactly this anxiety and confusion which makes us all 'normal'.

After all it's normal to wake up sometimes and hate the way you look, normal to be in a bad mood now and again, and very normal to have doubts about yourself. Part of becoming an adult is learning that you don't have to fit into some perfect mould. As long as you're always honest to yourself and don't cause anyone else any harm, that's about as 'normal' as you can hope to be.

'So what's this book all about, then?' I hear you ask. Well, it's about not worrying. It shows you how to cope when your body shoots off in one direction and your mind in another. It points out that not having a boyfriend, fancying your best friend, or only having one parent, isn't the end of the world. And above all it makes it very clear that being a unique person, with your own special gifts and talents, is the most normal thing in the world.

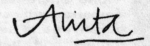

Contents

Chapter One

YOUR BODY

Dealing with your body is hard when you're a teenager. It's a time when your hormones go crazy, your body sprouts in various odd directions, and spots and pimples appear at the most inopportune moments. It's often made worse because everyone else seems to handle it with such ease. No one ever talks about how they're feeling wonderfully happy one moment and horribly inadequate the next. No one tells you they are worried because their periods haven't started or because something odd is happening to their breasts. And no one ever talks about all that strange body hair that appears practically over night! The truth is that our bodies are perplexing things and we're all too scared and embarrassed to mention it.

If there is one definite thing which can be said about the human body, it's that each and every one is completely different. We come in all different shapes, sizes, lengths, widths and colours. Some of us have short noses, others long. Some of us feel too fat, others too thin. And despite what you think, no one is ever 100% happy with their bodies.

Let's face it, our bodies are hugely important in our lives. They affect our everyday existence and our emotions. Other things about us are important too, like what we do with our lives and how we behave towards other people. But one thing's for sure - if we don't come to terms with the bodies we have, and learn to use them the best way possible, we can never be truly happy.

This chapter is about how to deal with your feelings towards all those bits you think you hate. Remember, however much you hate your small breasts/hands/nose, or loathe your large bottom/lips/feet, they are part of you and who you are. You may think no one will ever like you because of them, but the fact is that beauty is very much in the eye of the beholder. What's unappealing to one person is hugely desirable to another.

Are yours too big, too small, too droopy or too flat for your liking? I have a friend who hated her breasts when we were teenagers. When we were 13 years old she spent hours wishing for some miracle to make them grow, so she could look like the rest of us - but nothing happened. Yet when she reached 15 years old, her body suddenly started developing and before she knew it she had the biggest chest in our class. Was she happy? No, of course she wasn't! She then spent the next five years of her life complaining about her ample bosom and blaming her breasts for everything that went wrong in her life. It's only now, at the age of 23 years old, that she's come to terms with the fact that her breasts are just breasts and don't affect her life in the way she's always thought. The moral of this tale is that you shouldn't waste ten years of your life hating a part of your body that is perfectly natural and normal. Remember, breasts are like any other part of your body - they are made up of fat and tissue - and that's all. They don't have the ability to make you unhappy unless you choose to focus upon them.

Having breasts is a perfectly normal part of being a woman. Yet many of us learn to feel insecure about it because of the emphasis that TV, advertising and films puts on breasts. The models we see on TV and in magazines often have the most remarkable breasts. Either they are completely flat, incredibly large, or exactly the same size. And what's more, most of them stay perpetually perky no matter what they do! These models are either naturally thin women with their own normal breast size or women who have paid huge amounts of money for 'perfect' breasts through cosmetic surgery.

Of course, this leaves the majority of us feeling pretty insecure about our own breasts. Not many of us want breasts that bounce when we move, droop when we don't wear a bra, or refuse to fit even into the smallest cup. But the important thing to remember is that all breast sizes are normal, all nipples come in different sizes and colours, and that all breasts move when you walk. Even if you think your breasts are abnormally large or pitifully small, nine times out of ten they will be the perfect size for the type of body you have. If you're still not convinced, here are a few of the most common worries about breasts.

❝My breasts are too big.❞

The question is how big is BIG? For some girls being a B cup seems big, while for others a DD, or even an F, cup is their idea of being large. The fact is there is no such thing as a 'normal' bust size. Of course, it's difficult if all the girls in your class are flat chested and you're not. Or if the boys in your class make fun of you. But I can tell you now, most of the girls are bound to be more than a little bit jealous of you, and most of the boys are just too immature to deal with changing bodies.

Bust size is partly hereditary. If your mother hasn't got as large a chest then it may be your grandmother or an aunt who has passed it down to you. Time is also another factor, as your breast size will actually fluctuate until you are 16 or 17 years old. This is the age when you reach the final stage of breast development. Your body weight can also be a factor in determining how big your breasts are. However, just because you lose weight it doesn't automatically mean your breast size will go down. Some girls do find their breast size reduces when they lose weight while some very overweight girls find they go from having fairly flat chests to having breasts when they lose excess weight from around the top of their body. You can help yourself by making sure you wear the right sized bra. Refusing to wear one, or squeezing yourself into a small one, will just make you look and feel terrible. Breasts need to be supported properly or else they will droop and become saggy. Go along to any major department store and make sure you are fitted by trained staff for a bra. Marks and Spencers, John Lewis and a variety of other stores will do this for free. This sounds highly embarrassing, but it's not. Firstly, you get to go into a private cubicle where a female member of staff will measure you beneath your breasts and across your breasts to determine your chest and cup size. Don't be embarrassed about baring all to a stranger, they see literally hundreds of breasts a day and, of course, they have breasts themselves. They'll measure you up so quickly you'll hardly notice a thing. ★

❝They call me pancake chest.❞

There is no set age for your breasts to start developing. Some girls start as young as 10 years old, while others don't start till they're 16 years old. Most girls find that their breasts start growing with the onset of puberty, at around 13 years old. You may not notice anything at first apart from a slight swelling and an odd twinge.

No devices or special creams can increase breast size, so don't waste your money. Remember, breasts are made up of body fat and glands, not muscles, so any exercises you do will only affect the muscles underneath your breasts. Having a small chest doesn't mean you're not sexy. Many models are pretty flat chested and most of them look great. Myths that men only like girls with big breasts are also utter rubbish. Any man who judges a woman on her breast size isn't worth dating anyway! ★

❝I have lop-sided breasts.❞

Despite what people think, breasts aren't exactly the same size. Each breast differs slightly from the other in the same way one eye differs in shape and size from the other, and one hand is slightly different from the other.

Just because we have two of certain body parts, it doesn't mean that they're meant to be identical. If you don't believe me, take a look at your face. Your eyes are a pair but most people have one smaller than the other. Sometimes when breasts are developing their size will vary greatly, but generally the smaller breast will eventually catch up and be of a similar size (though probably not exactly the same). In the meantime, wear a proper bra that is designed to accommodate growing breasts. Teen bras can be found in all department stores. ★

❝My nipples are inverted.❞

Inverted nipples are nipples which turn inwards rather than outwards, and both men and women can have them. The condition is caused by tissues within the breast binding the nipple down. There is nothing to be worried about if you have inverted nipples, because they are pretty common. Often when your breasts grow, or when you become pregnant, they will naturally turn out. If you are at all worried about having inverted nipples then you should see your GP, who can suggest how you should look after them and make sure they are free from infection. ★

❮I have really lumpy breasts.❯

Having lumpy breasts is very normal during puberty, when your body is growing. The important thing to realise is that some breasts are naturally more lumpy than others. A lump doesn't automatically mean cancer. In fact, breast cancer is very rare below the age of 30 years old. However, you should learn to be aware of your breasts and examine them regularly. This means checking your breasts every month. A good time to do this is just after your period has ended, or if you haven't started yet, make sure you do them at the same time every month. Relax when you check them, and remember, you are looking for something which is unusual for you. So the first time, note the size and shape of your breasts, the look of your nipples and the feel of your breasts. (They may well be lumpy - especially before a period - and there's nothing wrong with this). Each time you check them, see if they differ at all from the first time. If you notice something like a lump, or a thickening, or an unusual swelling, get it checked out by your GP. For further information contact The Women's Nationwide Cancer Control Campaign, who produce a free leaflet on how to check out your breasts. (You'll find their address at the back of this book.) Above all, remember that the majority of breast lumps aren't due to cancer. The procedure of checking them out is just to be on the safe side. However, it is very important to get any lump that hurts or is growing checked out by your GP as quickly as you can. ★

PERIODs

The strange thing about periods is that you spend months wishing for them to arrive, only to wonder why you bothered when they finally do! Even if you haven't started your periods yet, you're still likely to have heard about all the hassles that go with them. PMS, PMT, cramps, tampons, sanitary towels, discharges and menstrual cycles. It's these things that cause some people to still refer to periods as 'the curse'. However, they aren't that bad. Periods are a good indicator that your body is working healthily. They are a sign that your body is maturing, and that it is ready to cope with having a baby.

A period occurs each month, when your body prepares itself for a possible pregnancy. An egg (we're all born with thousands of them) is released from your ovaries once a month and travels down to your womb. This has been preparing for the arrival of the egg by lining its walls. If the egg is not fertilised (i.e. you're not pregnant) the lining will be flushed out. This is your period. It's a mixture of blood (only two to three tablespoons, though it looks like much more) and womb lining.

❝I am 17 and haven't started yet.❞

There is no 'normal' age for your periods to arrive. I know one girl who started at 9 years old and another at 17 years old. A girl's first period often comes soon after her breasts begin to develop and her pubic hair begins to grow. Though again, this very much depends on your own personal body clock. The exact time you begin will be dictated by your hormones and no one can tell you when that will be. ★

it's my life...

❝My periods are irregular.❞

For the first two years, your periods are likely to be irregular. You may also find that you have your first period and then don't get another one for a few months. This too is normal, because even though most periods have a cycle of approximately 28 days, periods can take time to regulate themselves. Your periods will probably fall into a regular pattern eventually, although some women find that their natural cycle continues to be irregular. Factors such as diet, stress and exams can also effect your periods and throw them off course so - unless you've had unprotected sex - you have nothing to worry about. ★

❝I have a strange discharge.❞

Most girls get a normal vaginal discharge. This is a clear and colourless fluid. Some girls find this changes to a small brown discharge a few days before their period. As long as your discharge isn't itchy or doesn't smell, this is fine. If it becomes at all smelly, thick or heavy, or you get an irritating, burning or itchy feeling, you must get checked out by your GP as you may have an infection. ★

❝I have terrible PMT and period pains.❞

Despite medical evidence to the contrary, some people still think that both PMT (pre-menstrual tension) and period pains are all in the mind. In fact, it is estimated that 90% of women suffer from them at some point in their lives.

Women who get PMT may find themselves suffering in the days just before their period from bloating, moodiness, spots, clumsiness, tearfulness and headaches - to name but a few symptoms. Some women find that making sure they eat lots of fresh fruit and vegetables helps with PMT, as does cutting out sugar and fizzy drinks, coffee and fatty foods. Taking Vitamin B6 or Evening Primrose Oil supplements may also help.

Period pains, or cramps, are thought to be contractions of the muscles in the womb as they push the lining out.

This can be helped by placing a hot water bottle on your stomach, which will help to relax the muscles. A slow digestive system can make an uncomfortable period seem even worse, so eating the right food regularly can help solve the problem. Choose high fibre foods like beans, potatoes, and wholemeal bread. Lots of women swear that taking exercise relieves period pain, as this releases endorphins - the body's natural painkillers. ★

❝I can't use tampons.❞

Most girls find tampons hard to use the first time they try them. This doesn't mean you are odd or have a strange vagina. Often tampons are hard to insert because the muscles in the vagina are too tense. If this is the case then stop and try again when you feel less anxious. It can be done with a bit of practice - but only try to insert a tampon when you're having your period, otherwise your vagina will be too dry.

Choosing the sanitary protection which is right for you can be a very stressful thing, especially when there are still a multitude of myths to deal with. The plain facts are that tampons have nothing to do with virginity, any girl can use them, and they are not dangerous (as long as you use them hygienically). However, some girls feel happier with towels, and this is fine too. Work out what is best for you by trying the variety of products available.

Some girls prefer tampons with an applicator, while others prefer the ones without.

If you choose to use tampons make sure you use the right absorbency (slender, normal or super) and change them every three hours. If they feel at all uncomfortable, or if you start to feel hot, sick or dizzy, remove them and tell your GP. This is because there is a rare illness called Toxic Shock Syndrome, which can arise from using tampons. Very few women are affected however, so you have little reason to worry. ★

❛My vagina is a strange shape.❜

Unlike other parts of our body, we are not used to looking at our genital area. This is why suddenly having to deal with your vagina can be scary and a bit horrible. I often receive letters at *Just Seventeen* from girls worried because their genitals don't resemble any of the diagrams shown in health books or on tampon leaflets. The important thing to realise here is that it takes time to get used to how your genitals look, and also that a diagram is just a basic drawing to give you an idea, not a representation of what's 'normal'.

Some girls find they have small outer lips to their vagina, others have big lips. Some girls may even find that the lips to their vagina hang down. This is just the same as having a big nose or a small one. We are all built differently and not designed to look the same.

Don't feel shy or embarrassed about looking at your genital area, it's important to get to know where everything is so you know your way around yourself. If you're confused about what certain terms mean, here's a quick guide to what's what down below.

VULVA - The whole external area which surrounds the vagina.

VAGINA - The vagina is inside the body and its opening can be found between the inner labia.

CERVIX - This is at the top of the vagina at the opening to the womb. During childbirth it expands to allow the baby to pass through, but usually nothing can get up inside it.

UTERUS - This is the medical term for the womb and is where a baby grows in pregnancy.

LABIA - The vagina has two sets of lips also known as labia - the lips are known as the outer and inner lips.

CLITORIS - The most sensitive organ in the genital area. It is about the size of a pea and is found above the place where the labia meet.

URETHRA - The small opening below the clitoris through which urine passes. ★

BODY hAir

Body hair is a strange thing. In some countries it is thought to be sexy, but in Britain it isn't seen as a particularly attractive thing.

As long as you keep yourself clean, and you don't mind it, there's no reason why you shouldn't just leave your body hair alone. However, many girls find that they don't like excess hair on their bodies and want to get rid of it. The best way to do this is to use one of four methods: shaving, waxing, bleaching or depilatory creams. Plucking can be painful and isn't always very effective, while processes like electrolysis are rather expensive.

WAX N'SCREAM

⟨I have a moustache.⟩

Excess facial hair can be an embarrassing problem for some girls. In fact, we are all covered in facial hair, although those with darker hair find that theirs shows up more and so is more of a problem. If you feel you have a moustache you can't live with, you could use a depilatory cream (available from a good chemist) to get rid of it. Always follow the instructions carefully and make sure you do a patch test first, to see if your skin can take the cream. Depilatory creams are not meant for the whole of your face and should only be used on a moustache, not on your cheeks. Never shave facial hair because you'll end up with stubble! Bleaching (facial bleach available from a chemist) can be a good method but, again, do a patch test first to see if you like the results. Waxing can also be done on the face but this can be quite painful. ★

⑥I have excess pubic hair.⑨

One sure sign of puberty is pubic hair. This is the hair that grows around the genital area. The hair will often be fine and soft at first but as time goes on it will become coarser and thicker. The hair grows most thickly on the pubic mound and often stretches up in a thin line towards the navel. It also follows the line of the top of your thigh, sometimes known as the bikini line. Some girls prefer to get rid of this bikini line hair as it shows when you wear a swimsuit. But again this is a personal preference. Remember, once you start removing hair anywhere on your body, it will always grow back. You will have to keep removing it every few weeks, depending on your hair growth. ★

BODILY FUNCTIONS

Our bodies give off a large amount of secretions and fluids - everything from saliva to sweat - without us even knowing. It's perfectly natural and normal, and nothing to be ashamed of.

❝I smell!❞

Body odour isn't particularly pleasant, but is very easy to end up with if you're not careful. Perspiration under the arms is completely normal but during puberty our sweat glands can go a bit wild. Sweating is simply one of the ways the body cools itself off. It becomes a problem when it dries on clothes you wear again and again. You can beat it by making sure you wash at least once a day, use an antiperspirant and wear clean clothes every day. Cotton clothes help reduce sweaty smells, while man-made products such as viscose and nylon encourage them. Don't worry about being the sweatiest person in class. Everyone perspires, and as your body matures the amount you sweat will also decline. ★

❝They say I have bad breath.❞

Lots of people have bad breath without even knowing it, and sadly only find out when they go to the dentist or if someone comments. If you're not sure, check to see if your tongue is always coated or if you constantly have a sour taste in your mouth. If you're really brave you could come right out and ask a very good friend to tell you the truth. Most bad breath is caused by tooth decay or a gum infection. If you think you have a problem with your teeth see your dentist for a check up. Make sure you clean and floss your teeth regularly and drink lots of water. Another cause of bad breath is diet. Make sure you have a healthy diet with lots of fresh vegetables and fewer refined foods like sweets and fizzy drinks. ★

❝I'm covered in spots.❞

Everyone from Cindy Crawford to Tom Cruise got spots when they were a teenager. Let's face it, hardly anyone escapes spots and pimples, because they are a part of being a teenager whether you like it or not. Spots have nothing to do with how clean or unclean you are. Research now shows that they aren't even caused by chocolate and sweets. Lots of spots, especially the red, lumpy ones known as acne, are caused by hormones - which is why lots of girls find they get more spots near to their periods. You can have acne on your back and chest as well as your face. But before you run off and hide in shame, bear in mind that over 70% of all teenagers get acne.

The good news is that acne often clears up of its own accord in a few years. Not much good now, I know, but you can help yourself in a number of ways. Firstly, don't pick or squeeze your spots. Not only does this spread them, it also makes them worse and causes scarring. By all means cover them up, but use your make-up sparingly. It can make your spots worse, so make sure you wash all your make-up off each night. Don't waste your money on those miracle spot products; they are only a temporary solution and can make your skin worse by drying it up and stripping it of its natural defences. Your best bet is to see your GP. Acne is, after all, a medical condition and you can be given antibiotics to fight it. Don't give up on the treatment, as it often takes up to six months to work, because it'll be well worth it in the end.

Try not to get worked up about your spots because stress and worry can make your acne worse! Unfortunately students often find their acne flares up around exam time. ★

Chapter TWO

YOUR FAMILY

The ideal families we often see on TV never argue, never fight and always love each other. But in real life no family, however close, can live up to this image. It's in the very nature of human relationships that we argue more when we care and live closely with people we love.

All families come with their own in-built stress factors. They have the capacity to make you madder than hell and happier than anything else on earth. Yet, love them or hate them, they are yours for life. The important thing to remember is that no two families are ever the same. Not everyone comes from a two parent family made up of a father and a mother. Some people's families are made up of one parent, others have three or more parents, some people live with guardians, others with a relative and some live with parents of the same sex. It doesn't matter what kind of family you have as long as they love you and you love them.

Of course, it isn't always easy to love someone who makes your life hard, someone who hassles you for seemingly ridiculous things, and stops you from having fun. It's also difficult to love someone who has problems that affect your life and so become yours too, through default. It's especially hard to live with parents who are no longer in love and use you as a weapon against each other. This is why it's important to realise that there's no such thing as 'normal' parents. They aren't supposed to be perfect. They are people who, just like you and I, make mistakes, wrong decisions and overreact.

Learning to see that your parents are fallible human beings who don't always know the right thing to do is all part of growing up and becoming an adult - as is learning to communicate with them. At the same time, no matter what your parents might say, standing up for yourself and what you believe in (even if it's against their wishes) is also normal. Learning to handle your family successfully is good preparation for life. It will help you deal emotionally and physically with other relationships, so giving you a solid basis upon which to live your life.

❝My parents argue all the time.❞

All couples argue, even the ones who are madly and passionately in love. They fight because sometimes it's impossible not to be driven crazy by someone you love. Of course, even if you know that arguing is normal, it isn't particularly nice if you have to live with it every day. However, having said this, it isn't normal behaviour if your parents scream or hit each other. But then it isn't because of you, either. Just because some parents fall out of love with each other it doesn't mean they are going to fall out of love with you. You need to realise that your parent's happiness is their responsibility and if they choose to make each other unhappy then that's their problem.

Of course, if it gets you down to the point where you stay away from them or hide in your room, you have to talk to them. Get your worries out in the open and see if you can make them change their ways. If this doesn't work, you have to accept that their problems are their own and try not to get involved. Don't let them make you take sides, and don't try to be the mediator. ★

❛I don't get on with my family.❜

Throughout all the years of being a teenager myself and then dealing with teenagers' letters, I have never found one person who got on with their parents all of the time. In fact, when I was a teenager my father's most repeated phrase was, 'What happened to the lovely girl you once were?'. My typical surly answer was, 'She grew up.'

Most parents have a pretty hard time dealing with their kids when they are growing up. Suddenly their cute kids who did everything they said and listened to their every word, now have thoughts of their own. Thoughts that don't always go hand in hand with their own. What's more, teenagers also want to experiment with their lives, do their own thing and make their own mistakes. For many parents this is all too much, and is the root of many a disagreement.

Of course, many of us don't make our lives easier by being secretive and lying about what we are doing. If you don't get on with your parents because they are too nosy about your life you need to ask yourself why they are like this. It's not because they want to know exactly what you're doing at every moment of the day, it's because they are trying to protect you. Try not to take everything they say as a potential insult and don't be defensive every time they say something. If they are hurtful, pull them up on it. Point out that they wouldn't say that to their friends, so they can't say it to you. Remember, your parents need to realise that you are your own person with your own feelings and thoughts, as well as their daughter or son. ★

❝I found their pornographic magazines.❞

Pornography is an emotive subject. Some people feel it encourages attacks against women and children while others say it fulfils an important sexual need for adults. The fact is that it's legal, and although pornographic material is used by some attackers, it's also used by many perfectly normal adults. Just because your parents have pornographic material in your house doesn't mean they are odd or perverted. Far from it.

Remember, just as you like some privacy to your life, so do your parents. They don't know everything about you and you don't know everything there is to know about them. They are separate people with their own needs and desires, just as you are.

Of course, it isn't easy to see your parents as sexual beings and this is why it's especially hard to deal with things like 'adult' magazines and videos. However, you need to realise that they are consenting adults, and as long as they are not hurting each other or anyone else then you have to respect what they do in private.

If you want to stand against your parents using pornographic material, then go ahead. But first, ask yourself what it is that most revolts you about it. If it's the content, then fine. But make sure it isn't that the pornography you've found has driven home the fact that your parents are sexually active. Lots of people buy adult magazines, videos and sex aids, and as long as your parents aren't leaving them around or flaunting them at you, you have no right to say they are abnormal. Respect your parents' privacy and they will respect yours. ★

'I'm jealous of my sister/brother.'

Jealousy is a natural, but dangerous, thing. It eats away at our self-confidence and makes us feel weak and useless. Often, the first time we experience this emotion it's about one of our siblings. I remember being jealous about each of my brothers in turn. I was jealous because one was very clever and got all my parents' praise, and jealous of the other because my parents were always encouraging him to do better. Caught in between, I was convinced that I must be pretty rubbish at everything because my parents rarely said anything about what I was doing.

It was only years later that my mother told me she didn't say much to me at the time because she was too afraid I'd do the opposite of whatever she said. Likewise, a close friend of mine always hated her older sister for being exceptionally pretty. Rather than discuss it with her sister, my friend took her feelings as a sign that she was abnormal and ugly. She let her jealousy destroy her self-esteem for years and years. As a result, the two sisters were never close. When my friend went away to university she and her sister finally became closer, and ironically, one day, her sister turned round and admitted she'd always been jealous of my friend! They laugh about it now but both find it pretty sad that they wasted so many years.

The answer to feelings of sibling jealousy is to admit to them. You never know what you may find out in return, and being honest will help you to get your feelings into perspective. Remember that just because you're different, it doesn't mean that one of you is better than the other. ★

❢ My parents/brother/sister attack me!❣

No one has the right to hit and abuse you, no matter who they are. If you are being frequently attacked by a sibling then speak to your parents and get them to step in. Fighting back often achieves nothing so don't spend your days plotting how to get back at them. Getting an adult to deal with it is your best line of action.

If it's your parents who are abusing you, you must seek help now. There are a number of agencies and help organisations who will give you free confidential help and advice. Try to keep in mind that you are not alone, that whatever's happening is not your fault, and that your parents are not allowed to attack you either verbally or physically. The NSPCC, Childline or your local Social Services (you'll find the number in your local directory) can and will help you. ★

❢ I keep running away...❣

It's completely normal to hate your life at times. There are always going to be days when you wake up and hate everything. However, running away all the time isn't a solution and it won't solve a thing. If you're someone who thinks life would be better if you lived somewhere else, or away from your parents, think again! We all

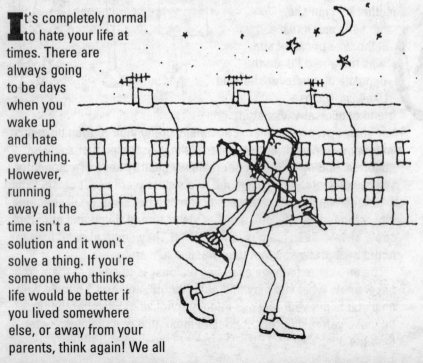

have things we blame for the bad things in our life. For some it's a bodily feature, for others it's a person or a place. We then use this thing and say, 'If only I didn't have to live here or live with them or have this long nose... my life would be wonderful.'

The fact is that running away solves no problems because we are trying to run away from ourselves. Wherever we go, we can't achieve this. If you're someone who keeps running away or thinking about it, try discussing your problems with someone you trust. This will help you to learn to deal with the things that worry you rather than trying to push them away. ★

⑥They hate my friends.⑨

Do you like all your parents' friends? I know I don't! And what's more, I don't expect them to like all of mine. If your parents have a real problem about one of your friends then you need to ask yourself if they've got a valid reason or if they are just being unfair. Someone who is known for being in trouble with the police, or for drinking or taking drugs won't exactly inspire confidence in parents. However, if all the talk is pure malicious gossip then stick up for your friends. Don't yell and scream, but quietly point out that your parents should at least give your friends a chance. If they refuse then you have a choice. You can either meet your friends somewhere other than your home, or you can stand your ground. You have a right to pick your own friends and use your own judgement to decide if they are bad or not. Your parents can't protect you from everything, and some things you need to discover for yourself. ★

⑥Why are they so over-protective?⑨

We live in a dangerous world where people go missing all the time. We hear about rapes, murders and senseless muggings every day on the news. Bearing this all in mind, it's not hard to see why a lot of parents can over-react and become too protective. It's a normal response to the horrors of life.

There are, however, ways round this. If your parents are too protective, make sure you don't give them reason to distrust you. Lying about where you're going, coming home two hours late, and hanging about with known trouble makers, won't help you prove to them that you can be trusted and can take care of yourself.

If you're mad at your parents because they won't let you out late, then talk to them about it. Try and reach a compromise, like you promise to be in by 9pm during the week if they let you stay out later at weekends. Contrary to what you think, your parents don't interrogate you just to ruin your life. They do it because they are worried and want to make sure you're safe. Instead of making every question into an ordeal, remember that the quicker you answer their questions, the quicker you'll be on your way. ★

❝My parents embarrass me.❞

Having embarrassing parents can be the worst thing in the world when you're a teenager. But the strange thing is that no one else's parents ever seem to be cringe-worthy except your own.

In fact, everyone gets embarrassed by their parents. I have friends who tell stories of walking five paces in front of their parents so no one would know they were part of the same family! Or being mortified when their parents turned up for Open Day at their school wearing ludicrous outfits.

I remember one friend who had a very glamorous mother - she hated the fact her mum wasn't 'normal' like other mums. Meanwhile, we were all dead jealous that her mum was so fashionable!

The fact is even if you don't like everything about your parents there is nothing you can do. They are yours, warts and all. So try to learn to put up with their embarrassing characteristics, because they put up with yours. ★

❝One of my parents doesn't want to know me.❞

We're all bought up to believe that our parents should love us and want us forever, but sadly some adults just aren't capable of this. Whether for emotional, financial or practical reasons, not everyone has two parents who love and care about them. The important thing to realise is that your parents' behaviour is in no way a reflection on you. So rather than making excuses for them, you have to see that their behaviour is their problem and their weakness. Just as you can't force another person to love you, you can't make a person take responsibility if they are ultimately irresponsible.

Don't waste your time thinking, 'If I were a better person they would have stuck around.' Unfortunately, some people who have children can't cope with having to be responsible. One in four marriages end in divorce, so the chances of being in a one parent family is high. If you worry that one parent doesn't love you, try talking to the one you feel closest to. They will reassure you that a delinquent parent is no fault of yours. ★

❝ My mother/father says they're gay.❞

When most gay parents 'come out', they don't expect you to applaud their decision, then carry on as if nothing had happened. Most will have thought a lot about the worries and fears you will experience as a result. Choosing to come out is a hard decision, but it's better than living a lie. Imagine having to hide your true self for years and years and never being able to tell anyone how you really feel. This is exactly how gay parents feel who have not yet come out.

But remember that your parents are no more a reflection of you than you are of them. If people choose to dislike you just because one of your parents is gay then that's their problem, not yours. Hating a parent because they're gay is rather like cutting off your nose to spite your face. After all, they are the same person they were before they came out, and they always will be, no matter what their sexual preference. ★

My parents are racist.

If your parents have always been racist and still don't see sense, there may be very little you can do to change their views. It is very hard to reason with racist people - let alone change their minds - because there is no sense behind their beliefs. Your only option is to be true to yourself. You know what's right and what's wrong and you have to live your life accordingly. ★

My parents are splitting up.

Separation happens all the time, sometimes for many reasons, sometimes for no reason at all. Remember, your parents will always be your mother and father, whether they choose to stay together or not. If they do choose to separate it will be hard, but in time you'll see that they're better people when they are not hurting each other. Forcing your parents to stay together when they obviously don't want to would be unfair to everyone - including yourself. You deserve to grow up in a house where people don't fight, and your parents deserve to be happy too. Talk to them and tell them how much their separation frightens and worries you. Let your parents reassure you that just because they've fallen out of love with each other, it doesn't mean they'll fall out of love with you. ★

Chapter Three

LOVE

hat is love? What exactly is that complicated emotion which most of us think about every day of our lives? Is it red roses, presents and soppy songs? Or is it something else altogether?

Love is, in fact, something different for everyone. Unfortunately, we are constantly being told by films, TV and pop songs how love is supposed to feel. And it's because of all this hype that most us can't wait to throw ourselves head first into the arms of someone who isn't quite right for us. We're often led to believe that if we're not 'in love', or if we're single, there's something not quite right about us. As if somehow having a boyfriend makes us better and more attractive people. Ideally, we should all be too sensible to fall for this, but unfortunately peer pressure can sometimes force us to conform and settle for something we're just not happy with. There is no reason to have a boyfriend unless you meet someone you really fancy. And remember, if you date someone and they aren't right for you, you can back out any time you want. If you're still not sure about what's a bad reason for having a boyfriend, check out this list.

bad reasons for wanting a boyfriend

1 Your friends have all got one.
2 Having a boyfriend will give you something to do on Saturday nights.
3 You want to lose your virginity.
4 Having a boyfriend will make you feel attractive.
5 Having a boyfriend will give you something to show off about.

A s the old saying goes, we have to kiss an awful lot of frogs before we can find our Prince Charming. So, unless you're very lucky you won't find the person who's right for you until you've tried a few out. This is what relationships are all about: discovering who you are and what you'll put up with. Often it's the most painful and messy relationships which teach us the best lessons about ourselves. So whether you've had your heart broken or have yet to fall for anyone - don't give up. Love comes to us all in the end (whether you're looking for it or not!) so don't waste time worrying about it.

BOYS, BOYS, BOYS!

'I've never had a boyfriend.'

I receive at least a hundred letters a week from worried girls. Some of these girls are 12 years old, others are 17, but they all have one thing in common - they think they are odd because they're single. But what's wrong with being single? It isn't a reflection on the kind of person you are. It doesn't mean you're unattractive, and it doesn't mean you're never going to be in love.
In fact it doesn't mean anything at all.

Statistically your chances of getting a boyfriend are extremely high, but just because a girl in your class has already had ten boyfriends while you've had none, it doesn't mean you're a lesser person in any way. Some girls spend the whole of their teens going from boyfriend to boyfriend, while others find themselves single. But that's not the way it's always going to be. I know at least two girls who didn't get their first boyfriend until they were 19 years old, and they've been dating ever since. When it comes to love there are no hard and fast rules. If you're desperate for a boyfriend then you need to ask yourself why. Are you hoping that a boyfriend will solve all the problems in your life? Do you think that having one will make you less lonely? Or more attractive? Or more acceptable to your friends? If any of these are your reasons, you need to think again. Boyfriends are supposed to be a bonus in life, not your whole reason for living. Of course, it's hard to believe this when everywhere you look people are paired up, but relying on someone else to improve your life is a recipe for disaster. If you concentrate on making the best of yourself and your life, you will automatically become more attractive. Boys, after all, are attracted to girls who like themselves. No one wants to date someone who doesn't smile, has nothing to say and has no interests.

So don't waste your life worrying that you'll never get a boyfriend. Of course you will! And what's more, once you have one, you'll wonder what all the fuss was about. ★

'I keep two-timing my boyfriends.'

Going out with someone isn't always easy. It's even harder when you're not sure why you're actually going out with them in the first place. The pressure to have a boyfriend can sometimes be so great that it can persuade us to stay with someone who isn't really right for us in the first place. There are certain warning signals that let you know when you should re-think your relationships. If you're someone who keeps having affairs or kissing other boys when your boyfriend isn't around, it's likely that you're either with the wrong boy or not really ready for a relationship. The best way to determine this is to take time out on your own. Instead of lying to your boyfriend, suffering from guilt and thinking you must be abnormal to behave this way, give yourself some time and space. People who have affairs do so because they aren't ready to commit to one particular person. It doesn't necessarily mean they don't love the person they are with, it just means they don't love them enough to give up everyone else.

Being single isn't as bad as you may think. It gives you the freedom to flirt with anyone you want, to get close to whoever you want and to spend your time however you like. Staying with a boy just because your friends are pressurising you to, or because you're afraid of being alone, is unfair to yourself and to your boyfriend. If you're still not convinced, then imagine how you'd feel if the tables were reversed. If in doubt, always treat someone the way you expect to be treated yourself. ★

⑥I only fancy older men.⑨

Older men are attractive, aren't they! They are more sophisticated, more sexy and better at chatting you up. And so they should be - they've had more practice. But surely age doesn't matter when you're in love, does it? Unfortunately when you're under 18 it does. Maybe not to you, but definitely to your parents and everyone else you know. No one can blame you for fancying older men because they're often more attractive than boys your own age. However, older men are bad news.

Apart from the little details - like older men are usually married or engaged or have a steady girlfriend - whether you like it or not, they are in a completely different league to you. Of course, it's very flattering to be pursued by an older man and it's tempting to date them. But a lot of your interests and friends will naturally be completely different.

If you find that you only fancy older men, ask yourself why. Is it because they have more money or glamour? Is it because dating an older man will impress your friends? Or is it because dating an older man gives you more confidence and makes you feel more attractive? If it's any of these reasons then you need to reassess your attitude to relationships. Perhaps you aren't quite ready for one yet. A boyfriend is not a possession to show off and boast about. Dating is about liking someone's personality, not their age, car, job or house. ★

❝Boys don't like me the way I am.❞

Pretending to be something you aren't is a recipe for disaster. If a boy doesn't like 'the real you' then there's no point going out with him. Relationships are hard enough without the pressure of having to be something you aren't. You are who you are, and you should never change for anyone. Anyway, just because a boy likes certain things, it doesn't automatically mean he wants his girlfriends to like them too. Having things in common is great, but having different interests can make a relationship just as exciting. ★

❝I prefer crushes to real boys.❞

Often the first person with whom we fall in love is someone we hardly know or have just seen on TV or in a magazine. They are often a first step into love and a 'safe' way of learning how to deal with all the ups and downs of a relationship. Some girls go through loads of crushes before they actually decide they want a boyfriend. If you're someone who has crush after crush, don't worry. There's nothing wrong with you. As long as you're happy and it's not driving you to tears then that's fine.

If it's upsetting you, then you need to bring your crush back down to earth. Try to keep it fun. Don't drive yourself mad with jealousy every time you hear he's with someone else. Spending all your time dreaming about him will just make you more upset and frustrated, so try to set aside a certain time in the day to talk and think about him. Most importantly, don't feel you're being cheated out of a relationship with him. This is the number one cause of most misery in crushes. Above all, be realistic.

Your crush is partly based on what the person looks like, and partly on what you've read or heard about them - not what you actually know from being face to face with them. The fact is, people in the flesh are very different from how you imagine them to be. For instance, if someone had convinced themselves that you were the one for them after seeing a picture of you, reading your biography, and watching you on video, you'd think it a bit strange, wouldn't you? No matter how much you know about a person, you can never really be in love with them until you meet them.

Even then, it takes a long time to get to know someone properly.

This is not to say that your attraction isn't real. It is. But you have to keep your feelings in perspective, otherwise you will drive yourself crazy. What's more, don't dismiss all the boys you do know. They may not be able to live up to your crush, but they're much easier to get hold of! You may not fancy them now, but one day you will. After all, it's no fun kissing a poster! ★

⑥My boyfriends always leave me...⑨

Thanks to the world of film and TV we are taught from a very early age that when you find love it lasts forever. Unfortunately, that's a load of rubbish. Love doesn't always last forever, especially first love. This is because love changes as we do, and sometimes we have to let go of a person who used to be right for us, but sadly isn't any more. Relationships, even very good ones, often reach a point where they can no longer go on. Sometimes, this is because one person starts taking another for granted or one person falls out of love with the other. In fact, no relationship stays the same forever. The first exciting throes of love always change, and either become something more long lasting or fade away.

If you're someone who's always on the receiving end of broken relationships, don't take it as a sign that you're no good. Remember, you're still the same person your boyfriends fell in love with. The only thing that has changed is their perception of you. This doesn't mean that you're never going to meet the right person, or have a long lasting relationship. All it shows is that particular person was wrong for you.

Being rejected is a painful and horrible part of love. But it's not a terminal condition. With time, heartbreak does lessen and you will find someone else to love. Don't think that you're never going to give another person a chance ever again. Love does hurt but, at the end of the day, the pleasure always outweighs the pain. ★

The Practical Perils of Love

❝I can't kiss!❞

OK, who hasn't practised kissing their pillow or their hand, hoping that when it comes down to the real thing they'll be ready? Well let me put your mind at rest, there is no right or wrong way to kiss. Kissing comes naturally as long as you follow three main rules.

1. Always relax. Try not to tense up when someone tries to kiss you. Don't worry if your noses bump, or you miss his lips, or it gets a bit sloppy.

2. Always kiss someone you like! Obvious, I know, but 90% of people say they can't kiss, or that their boyfriend has told them they can't kiss, because they're kissing someone who is completely wrong for them. If someone tries to kiss you and you don't want to, don't go along with it. Stand your ground and push them off. Likewise, if your boyfriend tells you you can't kiss, ask yourself what you're doing with him! Kissing is a two way thing, and it takes more than one person to mess it up.

3. If your kiss hits his cheek instead of his lips, or his nose hits your forehead, then don't give up in despair - try again. Part of the fun with kissing is practising with a person you really like.

If it's french kissing you're worried about, worry no more! All this means is using your tongue when you kiss. What usually happens is you and your boyfriend open your lips when you're kissing and put your tongues into each other's mouths. This sounds revolting at first, but it can be very pleasurable. However, it is a very intimate form of kissing and has a high chance of being a yucky experience if you do it with someone you don't really like! ★

❛I can't say 'I love you'...❜

'I love you', must be three of the most over-used words in the world, and it's for this very reason that lots of people feel stupid about saying them. However, there are also a number of other reasons why they sometimes refuse to come out of our mouths. Love is such a strange thing that many of us don't even know for sure when we're really feeling it. Often we feel pushed into saying it because it's expected of us. For instance, when our friends keep asking us if we're 'in love', or if our boyfriend says it and we feel obliged to say it back.

If you can't say it, then ask yourself these questions. Is it because you're not sure if you're in love or not? Is it because no one ever said it in your house when you were growing up? Or is it because you feel it sounds stupid?

If you answered 'yes' to the first question, give yourself some time.

Just because someone says it to you, it doesn't mean you have to say it back. When you're sure, you'll feel ready to say it.

If you can't say it because you've never had to before, then don't worry - with a bit of practice, you'll be able to do it. Saying 'I love you' takes courage. Its implications are huge, and if your family don't openly show or talk about their feelings it may take you longer to work up the courage. But don't give up. When you trust someone enough, you'll say it.

Likewise, if the phrase sounds stupid to you, just give yourself time to get used to it.

Anyway, there are more ways than one to say 'I love you' and as long as you show that you do, in time you'll find yourself saying it without even realising it. ★

❝I can't ask him out.❞

Thankfully, gone are the days when girls had to sit around and wait for a boy to ask them out. However, this doesn't stop some girls from thinking that it's a boy's job to do the asking. If you feel this way, think about how a boy must feel.

Asking someone out is a scary business. It means you have to put yourself on the line and open yourself up to rejection. (Horrible stuff when you think about it!) Contrary to popular belief, boys aren't born with an in-built mechanism that enables them to do this. They are just as scared and unsure as the rest of us. But, thank goodness, they've been doing it for years - otherwise where would we all be?

However, not all boys ask girls out. I have one friend, Robert, who has never asked a girl out in his life. He is good looking and friendly, but too shy to believe that a girl would like him. He therefore has no self-confidence when it comes to asking girls out. Plenty of girls have fancied him but none have gone out with him because none have had the courage to do the asking. He is now going out with a girl he works with and they are very happy. How did she get him? Easy - she asked him out! It was that simple!

The moral of this tale is that if you want something, you should go for it. It's no good sitting about and waiting for a boy to approach you. If you like someone, ask them out! The worst he can say is 'no' and that's not as bad as you might imagine. If he isn't interested, then at least you can give him up and go after someone else. It's better than sitting at home and wondering whether or not he likes you.

And just because he doesn't ask you out, it doesn't mean he's not interested. Boys are just the same as us. They are just as scared, unsure and unconfident about their looks and abilities. If you want to get a boy's attention, then just treat him the way you'd treat a girl friend. Talk to him the way you'd talk to anyone else and don't expect him to always take the lead. ★

❛He doesn't fancy me!❜

Unfortunately, if someone doesn't fancy you there's not much, if anything, you can do to change their mind. Attraction is a mysterious thing; no one really knows why we fall for some people and not for others. On top of this, the intensity of feelings that often accompany a physical attraction always makes rejection even more painful to bear. The only thing you can do is give yourself time to get over rejection. After all, heartbreak is heartbreak whichever way you look at it. ★

❛I can't get over him.❜

If you can't get over your ex, it could be because you would rather be unhappy about him than not think about him at all. Lots of people do this when they are heartbroken, because they know that when they let go of the pain they are admitting their relationship is really over, once and for all. Lethargy, sadness, weight loss and personality change are all typical of someone who has slipped into a serious depression over a broken relationship. If you feel this way, you may need counselling to find a way out and get over what has happened. Your GP can find you a counsellor or you can contact Childline. ★

❝My ex hates me because I broke up with him.❞

Rejection is a hard thing for many people to take. Most of us deal with it by crying on our friends' shoulders and moping about, before finally getting on with life. Unfortunately, a few people aren't so controlled about it. These people have to learn that love doesn't come with guarantees and that part of going out with someone is taking the risk that it may not last forever. If you have an ex-boyfriend who is continually nasty to you because you ditched him, confront him. He has to realise that he can't bully and abuse you just because you were honest with him. At the end of the day if he can't handle rejection, he shouldn't go out with people. ★

❝He won't let me wear make-up.❞

You should NEVER let a boyfriend rule your life. If you want to wear tight clothes and make-up then that should be your choice, not his. These things aren't a sign that you're a tart or trying to chat up other men. They are a sign that you're a normal girl who likes wearing nice clothes and using cosmetics. If this is happening to you, you need to talk to your boyfriend and stop him trying to take over your life. Tell him that you wear these things for yourself and not for anyone else. Standing up for yourself, and what you want, is very important - otherwise he'll just keep putting more and more restrictions on your life. ★

‘ He hits me! ’

Men who beat their girlfriends and wives come from all areas of life and aren't like the stereotypes you see on television. The latest figures concerning men who beat their partners show that most women stay for an average of sixty attacks before they leave! Don't let yourself become one of these women.

Women who are attacked by their boyfriends are in NO way to blame for what happens. If it's happening to you, get out of the relationship as quickly as you can. If he won't leave you alone, tell your parents, your friends and the police. Whatever you decide to do, remember he isn't just going to stop attacking you. So leave him before it gets any worse. ★

Chapter four

FRIENDS

Boyfriends come and go, but good friends - if you're lucky - can last a lifetime. I can't say enough about the importance of friends. You may be someone who has only one good friend, or you may be someone who has lots of friends - it really doesn't matter as long as you realise how important they are. You can get by with almost anything except friends. Your friends are the only people guaranteed to be there when you're unhappy, broken-hearted or depressed. They are also the very people who will be there during the good times, to share your happiness.

Friendships are like any other relationships - you can't afford to take them for granted. You have to work at them, and even when they annoy you, you have to learn not to walk away. If any relationship is to be long-lasting, you have to work through the hard times as well as the good.

As for best friends - sure, it's great to have one, but it's not the answer to everything. In fact, it's better to have a number of different friends with whom you can share different interests, rather than one friend with whom you do absolutely everything. In any case, putting all your eggs in one basket can make you quite vulnerable. For a start, being seen as a twosome puts other people off being friends with you. But you also have to think about would happen if she moved away or you fell out - you'd have no one else to be friends with.

As for making friends, well, this is both the hardest and the easiest bit. You can make a new friend anywhere, not just at school or at a party. I have one good friend I met on a bus while I was in Italy, another I met through an ex-boyfriend and yet another I met when I went to take my driving test. So, you see, every time you meet someone you have a chance of making a new friend. As long as you smile and act friendly anything can happen.

Of course, there are going to be times when you and your friends fall out or grow apart, but this is perfectly natural and normal.

Relationships all change, no matter how much you fight to keep them the same. If you can grow together then fine, but if you can't, it may be time to call it a day. However, even though lots of people find as they get older they have less and less in common with their childhood friends, it doesn't mean they can't still be close. I have one very good childhood friend who I still meet up with, even though our lives are now completely different. I still treasure her friendship because we share so much of our past. But if you do break up with a friend you'll probably find that it's as traumatic as breaking up with a boyfriend. Loss of any kind needs to be grieved over and dealt with. You may need to work out your feelings of anger, but the most important thing to learn is not to dwell on people who have hurt you. If someone chooses not to be friends with you, for whatever reason (and sometimes there is no reason), then see it as their loss, not yours, and move on to friends who do like and love you.

Of course, it can be hard if a friend moves away. But as long as you make an effort to keep in touch, you can stay friends no matter how far apart you are. Obvious ways of keeping in touch are writing letters, sending funny postcards and maybe also telephoning now and again. Sometimes, in the excitement of everyday life, it can be hard to remember people who are not physically around. This is why it's important to make an effort with them.

Remember that friends are not just there for the good times. Collecting together a bunch of close friends will help you when you're feeling down. A good friend sticks by you in bad times just as much as good. They are there when you're having family problems, boyfriend break-ups or if you simply need a bit of cheering up. Likewise, you should do the same for anyone you care about - after all, that's just what friendships are about. ★

Making friends and keeping friends

❝I can't make friends.❞

Making friends is hard, especially if you happen to be shy. Sometimes it looks as if everyone else is having a wonderful time while you're left to hang about on the outskirts. But if you want to make friends, sitting about on your own isn't going to get you anywhere. Making friends and keeping friendships going takes a lot of effort and time. If you haven't got any friends for whatever reason, don't give up! There are a number of things you can do.

The first and most important thing is to decide who you want to be friends with. Finding someone who shares similar interests to you is important, because you need to make friendships with people that will reach further than your school boundaries. If you have a particular interest, you could join an after-school club to try drama or sports of some sort. This way you're guaranteed to meet someone you'll have things in common with.

If you haven't got a specific interest, there are other alternatives when it comes to making friends. But making the first move is always a good start. If you're particularly tongue-tied, then learn to ask questions. Most people find it very flattering to be asked questions about themselves, as it shows you're interested in them. Start by introducing yourself and then ask away. But remember to really listen to what they say. There's no use in questioning someone like crazy and then not taking in a thing they say! The whole point of asking someone about themselves is to work out what things you have in common and act upon them.

Another useful tip is to take the initiative when arranging to meet your new friend again. If Lucy mentioned she liked going to the cinema, then suggest you both go on Saturday, or if Helen likes window shopping, offer to go with her. It's only by giving people a chance to be friends that they'll give you one back.

It's also important to learn to give compliments (though not to the point where you become a creep!) and receive them. No one likes someone who doesn't like themselves. So if someone gives you a compliment learn to take it graciously.

Remember that making friends is a skill that can be learned, so don't give up. ★

❛She's started taking drugs.❜

If you have a friend who is doing something potentially dangerous to their health and they are out of control, you can do one of two things: ignore it - and hope it will go away, or take some positive action. Being a friend doesn't always mean doing exactly what your friend wants. If a friend is in danger, you MUST tell someone what's going on before they hurt themself. Imagine how you'd feel if a friend was injured because you were too scared to speak up. If they aren't going to seek help for themself, you need to speak for them. I'll be honest - they won't thank you for it, but it will be worth it in the end. For more information about how to help drug users contact ADFAM (you'll find their address at the back of this book). ★

❛She hates my boyfriend!❜

It isn't easy for close friends when one gets a new boyfriend. Suddenly friendship takes a second place and a friend can end up feeling used and rejected. Likewise, a boyfriend can feel left out and on the edge of a private joke. If you feel a friend has no reason to be jealous then be upfront and ask her why she's being so mean. At the same time reassure her that having a boyfriend makes no difference to your relationship. If you feel you've been a bit neglectful, be honest and make it up to her. After all, your best friend and your boyfriend both like you - so you should all be able to be friends! ★

Losing friends

❝My friend dumped me for her boyfriend...❞

Are you guilty of this? Are you someone who dumps your friends the minute a boy comes on the scene? If you are - shame on you! Friends are not fill-ins for when you are single. If you think this way, you're going to wake up one day without any friends at all. If you're in doubt about how to treat a friend, always treat them the way you expect to be treated yourself.

On the other hand, if you have a friend who always ditches you when a man comes on the scene, it may be time to put your foot down. Make it perfectly clear that you're happy she's happy, but you're not going to be a stop-gap for her. Perhaps she's so caught up in her excitement that she hasn't realised that she is treating you in a pretty mean way. If this is the case then a quick word here and there will put it right. If not, then now is the time to talk about it.

If you're someone who keeps getting ditched by a friend the minute a boyfriend comes on the scene, remember that what is happening is not a reflection on you but on your friend. Don't let her continually take you for granted. You deserve as much respect as her boyfriend, and if she can't give it to you, then you need to ask yourself just what you're getting out of this relationship. ★

❝My best friend bullies me.❞

Bullying is a terrible problem in Britain. We have the worst record of it in Europe, and while more obvious cases of playground bullying are now being addressed, a lot of cases still go undiscovered. This is because a lot of bullying is 'mental' and done by so-called 'friends'. Best friend bullying is, in fact, extremely common. Unlike other forms of bullying, when it occurs most people aren't really sure if it's happening or not, therefore they stay quiet about it. After all, best friends aren't supposed to be nasty to each other. It also feels humiliating to admit that a friend is hurting you. But bullying is bullying whichever way you look at it. You have to always remember that as the victim you are in no way to blame for what is happening. The only way you'll be able to stop it is by telling someone what's going on. If you're still unsure about what is happening to you, then write down everything your best friend does to you. Keep a diary of everything she does to upset you. This way you'll have evidence to show she has been nasty to you, and it's not all in your head.

Givus ya sweets!

Instead of blaming yourself for what's happening, you need to look at your friend's motives. Is she bullying you because she is jealous of you? Or is it because she's insecure? Sometimes, people put other

people down to build themselves up - not a very nice trait. Whatever her reason, don't let her get away with it. Studies have shown that bullying is completely destructive - it can ruin your self-confidence and self-esteem, and its effects can last far longer than a friendship. Talk to your other friends, your parents or another adult you trust. Do yourself a favour and get away from her. ★

❛I'm jealous of my friends.❜

It's natural in any friendship to be envious of your friends. After all, you like and admire them and strive to be like most of them. However, if the green eyed monster's got hold of you because your think your friend gets asked out more than you, or because you think she's prettier or cleverer or funnier, then tell yourself this: there must be something good about you or else she wouldn't be your friend.

Another point to remember is that friendships are supposed to be equal. If you feel you're a lesser person than your friend then you're doing her an injustice. She is friends with you because she likes and admires you, not because she feels superior to you.

If you feel your jealousy is ruining your friendship, speak to your friend about it. You may be surprised to discover she is envious of you too. Talking about it will help you to get your feelings into perspective. I remember having a bust-up with my best friend because she was behaving oddly towards me. It turned out she was jealous because she thought I had an exciting life with lots of travelling (because of my job). What she didn't know was that I was jealous of the fact she had a lovely boyfriend and beautiful house. Once we'd sorted that one out we had a good laugh about it and agreed that it was a case of the grass always being greener on the other side.

At the end of the day, no one wants to be friends with someone who doesn't think very much of themselves. It would be exhausting and demoralising to be around them. So practise being good to yourself first and the rest will come naturally. ★

❝I think my best friend is gay.❞

If the fact your friend is gay puts you off her, then you have to ask yourself just how much you really like her. If you're going to ditch her just because you're afraid of what people will say then you can't be much of a friend. Remember that her sexuality is no one else's business but her own. Whether she's gay or not, she is still the same person you've been friends with for years. If I were you, I would stop worrying about what she is or isn't and think about what being a friend really means. ★

❝She won't stop copying me!❞

Basically, friends who act like your shadow do so because they lack the confidence to make their own decisions. Annoying as it is, they are using you as their role model. Instead of getting annoyed and losing their friendship, what you have to do is talk to them and help them to find their own style and sense of self. They obviously admire you and think everything you do is right, so they'll listen to what you have to say. Tell them you don't like the way they copy you, and if they want help in finding what looks right on them, you're willing to help. As long as you make your position clear without being nasty, they'll soon be able to stop copying you. ★

CRITH FRIENDS LIKE THESE...

❝My friends don't get on.❞

It's horrible when you get your two most favourite people together and they just don't get on. After all, you like them both and share similar interests, so how come they don't? Well, most of us behave differently with different friends, but we sometimes only realise this when we get two sets of friends together. If this is happening to you, don't worry about it. Just because you've chosen these two people to be friends doesn't mean they automatically have to like each other too.

Sometimes, friends don't get on because of jealousy. Seeing that you're just as close with someone else can be hard for a friend who thinks they have something unique with you. If this is happening to you, don't play your friends off against each other. It isn't very nice to feel left out or less liked than someone else. A bit of reassurance is all you need to give to sort out this problem. Make sure you let all your friends know how much you like and admire them. This way they won't feel threatened when you introduce them to someone else you know. ★

❝I can't take a joke.❞

Some people always love to tease and unfortunately, some people always end up being teased. Once or twice, it can be quite amusing. But on the whole, it isn't much fun for the person being teased. To a certain degree it's normal to be able to laugh at yourself, but if your friends use you as the butt of their jokes all the time then you must stand up for yourself.

Constant teasing is a form of bullying and just as self destroying. If you're someone who thinks this is happening to you, then speak to your friends. Don't laugh along with their jokes, tell them straight out how much their comments hurt and ask them to stop.

If you feel you take everything to heart for no reason then you need to look at why you're doing this.

99.9% of people are insecure to some point or other. We all hate jokes being made at our expense, even the ones we know aren't true. However, the important thing to realise is the distinction between a hurtful and playful remark. If someone makes the same hurtful comment again and again the chances are, you're not being over-sensitive by admitting you're hurt. If a person continually puts you down (even if it's in a jokey manner) or uses you as the butt of their jokes, you have a right to be angry. But if you get upset every time a friend teases you about something little, you need to realise that they are not being serious. Learning to laugh at yourself is a sign of confidence. And remember, no one wants to be friends with someone who takes themselves so seriously that they can't laugh at their weaker points. ★

'They all shoplift...take drugs... smoke...'

Peer pressure is something we all suffer from. Fortunately, although it doesn't go away with age, your ability to stick up for yourself and what you believe in gets stronger. However, when you're a teenager it can get you into no amount of trouble - all because you don't want to be the odd one out.

When I was fourteen I hated being seen to be the 'square' just because I refused to skive off school, or smoke in the park at lunchtimes. I wasn't very happy about being left on my own at breaktimes but now I don't regret it at all.

But it isn't always easy to make a stand. Many people feel pressurised into everything from sex to breaking the law, all because their 'friends' won't let them be different. If you have a friend or a group of friends who are trying to encourage you to break the law, take drugs, or do anything else you don't really want to do, you have to face up to the fact that these people don't have your best interests at heart. Friendship is about accepting a person the way they are, even if they aren't like you. If a group of friends refuse to let you be yourself then you need to question whether or not they are really your friends in the first place.

Making someone get involved with drugs and alcohol isn't something a friend does. You can bet your life that they won't be there when you're in trouble, so stand your ground against them now. ★

'I think my friends hate me...'

If your friends are being bitchy and spiteful to you, ask yourself if you want to stick around? They obviously think their behaviour is pretty amusing and haven't even given it a thought that they are being spiteful. While this is no way for so- called 'friends' to behave, it is more common than you think. But this doesn't mean you have to put up with it. Stand up for yourself and tell them to be nicer to you. Remember, you have done nothing wrong, so don't let them treat you this way. If they haven't got the decency to tell you things to your face then they deserve your anger when you hear what they've been up to behind your back. ★

Chapter five

SCHOOL

School is a complete nightmare for many people. If you're not worrying about work pressure and exams, there are the teachers and the rules to deal with. In fact, anyone who says school years are the best years of your life, is lying. But before you throw your school uniform down in disgust and refuse to ever go back, I'd better just point out that school isn't completely useless. Your school years are actually some of the most important years of your life. This is the time when you learn how to deal with different sorts of people. It's also the time when you decide what you're good at and what you hate. But most of all, it's the time when you get to learn about things that will get you through the rest of your life.

It's basically up to you. You can spend the next five to seven years learning absolutely nothing and complaining every day, or you can make the best of it and learn what you can. The advantages of the last method include the fact that you're going to get a lot further in your life if you have a few exams behind you. It's easy to take the first route if you find your school work hard, but there are ways round this. Asking for help is the first step and speaking up when you don't understand something, is the second. You're at school to learn and your teachers are there to help.

Trying, or rather wanting, to digest all the facts that are thrown at you can be another problem. I used to hate geography; I never understood why I had to spend hours learning to map read when I thought I'd never use it. Now it's become one of the most useful things I've ever learnt to do. Another friend could never understand why we had to spend hours learning about fractions and statistics - now she works in music marketing and deals with statistics all day. The point is you never know where you're going to end up when you're older and therefore, you don't know what you're going to need and what you won't. If you don't want to do something academic with your life then fine, but even 'glamorous' jobs call on your past education to get you through.

Teachers with problems, problems with teachers

Dealing with teachers can be difficult, especially if they act as if they hate you, don't explain their lessons and never look interested. Most teachers really do want to help but, then again, not all teachers are good at their jobs. If you have a problem with a teacher, or you have a teacher with a problem, tell your parents or another teacher you trust. Don't let them hold you back. ★

Bla Bla Bla

Bla Bl

❝My teacher says I'll never amount to anything...❞

Sometimes, it can feel as if all that teachers want is to keep you down. I remember a friend telling her careers teacher she wanted to write. His reply was, 'Writers don't come from this kind of area. You'd be better off working in a bank'. Three books, one screenplay and numerous newspaper articles later she has proved him utterly wrong. Another guy I know said he wanted to be a doctor, only to be told that he wasn't clever enough. These days he spends his days working in India and Africa as a doctor for the Red Cross.

My point is that teachers know some things, but they don't know everything. Just because they can't see your potential doesn't mean you haven't any. If you really want to be something and no one believes in you, don't let it stop you. Go for it and don't look back. For although your teachers know their own subjects inside out, their experience of the world is limited. If they scoff when you tell them that you want to work in film or TV, it probably means they've never met any one who works in these fields. There isn't a particular type of person who works in TV, medicine, law or banks for that matter. People come from different backgrounds and succeed because they are determined and work hard. In the words of world famous boxer Mohammed Ali, 'Part of being a champion is believing in yourself when no one else does.' ★

❝I lied and told everyone I was dating my teacher.❞

The trouble with telling lies is that one lie always leads to another, and before you know it you're caught in the middle of a sticky situation. However, there is a way out - to tell the truth. If you don't want to do it for yourself, then do it for your teacher. A lie like this will ruin his life. Not only will he lose his job, friends, family and any future job as a teacher, he may also be arrested and put in prison. Compare this to what you'll have to go through if you tell the truth and you'll see that your only option is to say you've been lying. ★

6 My teacher makes passes at me. 9

This is a potentially dangerous situation. If there is a teacher who is making passes at you or making you feel scared, then you need to tell someone what is going on. Make sure you make a note of everything he has said and done. This way you can be clear when you tell your story. A teacher has no right to make sexual suggestions, hit or attack you in any way. If you feel at all threatened by a teacher's actions then either tell your parents or another teacher you trust. ★

6 My teacher hates me! 9

Do you have a teacher who calls you names, singles you out for no reason and basically makes your life a misery? Don't let them undermine your self-confidence and turn you into a quivering wreck. If they are making you so miserable that you are skipping school, you need to address the situation. This means recognising that your teacher is cheating

you out of a good education and may be even ruining your chances of a good career. Ask your friends whether they think this teacher picks on you or not and then tell someone what's happening. Again, your parents are your best bet as they can step in with authority and make sure the situation changes. ★

Work, Work, work

Yes, it's unfair that exams count. Yes, it's unfair that not everyone is good at exams and yes, it's even more unfair that non-academic people get left behind. But life is unfair sometimes and, believe me, it gets worse when you get out into the job market. This is why it's important not to give up - no matter how hard you find your school work.

Not everyone is naturally gifted at academic work. Some people are more practical, or find their talents later in life. But we're all good at something and just because you're not an 'A' student or near the top of your class doesn't mean you should give up on your work. Despite the emphasis on competition within the classroom, exams and school work are for yourself. You shouldn't compare yourself to anyone. It doesn't matter if you only score 50% in a test, you know in your heart if this is a good score for you. We're not all born to get 99% in exams and go to university, some of us have other talents that get us to where we want to go. If you don't think you've got any talents, think about your personal skills. Are you a good listener? Do you like people? Can you make people laugh? Are you good at drawing or writing? What about your shopping skills? I know it sounds ridiculous, but even your shopping skills could point you in towards a job as a fashion buyer, a marketing assistant or even a window dresser.

Schools are geared towards academic work and higher education, but this doesn't mean they can't help you if this area isn't for you. Ask your careers teacher for advice and a good general careers book. This way you can look in the index and see if there is anything you like the sound of. Your non-academic teachers for subjects like Art and PE can also prove helpful. Also check out the careers section in your local library and you'll find a wealth of jobs you may never even have known existed.

❝I can't take the pressure!❞

It isn't always easy to deal with work pressure. Apart from the pressure of the work itself, pressure can also come from your parents. If your parents push you all the time, or boast about your work, you need to tell them that they are stressing you out. There's nothing worse than trying to live up to someone else's expectations and failing. If you have parents who push you and bully you when you get low marks, talk to them. Perhaps they don't realise how hard they are pushing you or that you're already trying your best. ★

❝I hate PE.❞

For many girls PE, or physical education, is the all-time low point of school. If there isn't the showers to worry about, there's the humiliation of doing sport in front of loads of people who are better than you. PE puts many people off doing physical exercise for the rest of their life - but there is a point to it.

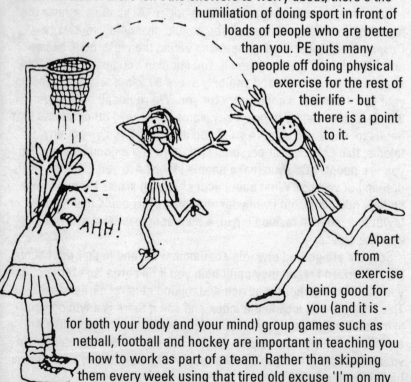

AHH!

Apart from exercise being good for you (and it is - for both your body and your mind) group games such as netball, football and hockey are important in teaching you how to work as part of a team. Rather than skipping them every week using that tired old excuse 'I'm on my period', make an effort to at least try at them. PE teachers are notorious for only giving high marks to girls that are good at sport, but as long as you feel you're giving it your best, that's all that counts. ★

❛I'm terrified of my new school!❜

Any new situation tends to cause some degree of anxiety in most people, and starting secondary school can be a terrifying time. Suddenly you're thrust into an environment that's huge, seemingly unfriendly and packed full of people. This is guaranteed to give you a fear about going there. Physical symptoms often include headache, nausea, stomach pains and shakiness - panic attacks, brought on by your fear of school. If it's so bad that you physically can't get to school, get your parents to talk to your teachers so they can give you work to do at home. This way you won't fall so far behind while you're trying to get over your fear. Also get your GP to write them a letter so they know you're not making up these attacks. Seeking professional counselling help through your GP will also help you to overcome your fear. ★

Bullying

Anyone who has ever seen someone being bullied, or who has been bullied themselves will know how terrifying and awful it is. Bullying not only destroys the self-confidence and self-esteem of victims, it also alienates them to such a point that they feel they are in some way abnormal.

Britain actually has the worst record for bullying in Europe and less is done here than anywhere else to combat the problem.

Bullying can have a lasting effect on the bullied person and many adults talk about how 'humiliated' and 'distressed' they still feel over events that took place over ten or twenty years ago.

Bullying itself is not a criminal offence, but the actions of a bully may well constitute a crime such as assault or theft. If you are being bullied, or know of someone who is being bullied, then you owe it to both yourself and them to tell someone what's going on. Bullying, and the way it is dealt with, will only change if more people speak up about it. ★

'Bullying has destroyed my confidence.'

Victims of bullying often feel useless. If you've been bullied, you have to convince yourself that this isn't the case. You have just been worn down over a long time by all the bullying you've suffered. Don't ever underestimate the effect bullying has on your confidence. Many people who were bullied at school still find themselves suffering from lack of confidence, shame and humiliation, years after the actual event. This is because bullies are very good at making their victims feel they are to blame for what is happening.

The fact is, if you're being bullied, you are the innocent one. Whatever you do, don't give up. Many people get over the after-effects of bullying by seeking help at one of the bullying self-help groups. Bear in mind that bullies thrive on their victims' silence, and that you owe it to yourself and others to tell someone what's happening. There are several organisations which specialise in helping you deal with bullies, including ABC (Anti Bullying Campaign), Childwatch, Kidscape and Childline. (You'll find addresses for all of these at the back of this book.) They also offer help and advice for parents. ★

'They bully me because I'm fat/short/too thin...'

There is no reason why people get bullied, although sometimes they are picked on because of obvious things such as skin colour, size or hair colour. People who are bullied because of these things often feel ashamed of themselves and humiliated, but it is the bullies who should feel ashamed, not the victims. Being different is something people admire as they get older, not laugh at. If you're being bullied, don't let the bullies humiliate you into thinking you're not as good as everyone else. These ignorant people need to learn that not liking someone because they are different is an abnormal and immature way to think. ★

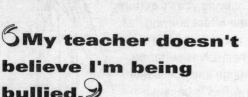

❝My teacher doesn't believe I'm being bullied.❞

Sometimes, telling can be hard, especially if you haven't got any witnesses. Teachers, parents and even friends can let you down when you most need them. The trick here is not to give up and keep on telling, until someone believes you. Eventually, someone will.

Unfortunately, despite all the information about bullying, some teachers are still totally useless when it comes to putting a stop to it. But they aren't the only people who can help. Get your parents to write to the school governors. The Local Education Authority can also help locate you to a new school. If the bullying is physical, or you have been receiving threats, then your parents should think about contacting the local police. ★

School friends

An important part of school isn't the lessons, but the people you hang out with. They can make or break your happiness and affect everything - from the amount of homework you do, to whether or not you pass your exams. If you're lucky, then you get to see your school friends out of school. But if you live too far for this to happen, or don't know anyone special at school, life can seem lonely and school life difficult.

❝I lied to my school friends...❞

If you start exaggerating what your life is like out of school - for whatever reason - it can lead you into no amount of trouble. A small lie can easily grow and grow and become huge before you know it. If you've told a lie at school about your home life, whether it's about your parents' house or your boyfriends, now is the time to stop. I'm not suggesting for one moment that you come clean, as telling the truth now will only add to your embarrassment. If I were you, I'd just stop talking about whatever it is you lied about. If anyone asks, just shrug and say as little as possible. ★

❝I'm so shy, I have no friends at school.❞

Who doesn't sympathise with this one? Being shy has more than its fair share of problems. However, in order to deal with this situation you have to look at what's happening from your classmates' point of view. Your silence probably makes them uncomfortable. It may also make them think that you're judging them.

In a way, you can't blame your classmates. They don't know you at all, because you haven't let them get close. The irony of this situation is that you probably won't talk to them because you don't think you're good enough, while they don't talk to you because they think the opposite. A simple way out of this is just to talk to them. You don't have to say anything smart or witty, just a plain, 'hi' would be fine at first. Small gestures like smiling when they look your way, or asking how they are, will actually go a lot further than you think. Friendships are made when two people decide to open up to each other. Until you do this you can't expect anyone to be friends with you. ★

❝They blame my friends for my bad school marks.❞

Parents are always quick to blame friends when you get bad marks. In fact bad school marks are the bane of many a teenager's life. Apart from having to go through a whole parental explanation and interrogation their answer is usually to ban you from ever going out again. If this happens to you, try not to go off the rails in fury. If you really think your friends are in no way responsible, talk to your parents. Take full responsibility for what you have done - or rather, haven't done. Explain that you are going to work harder and not go out with your friends all the time. Prove you are mature enough to keep to their rules and they'll feel more comfortable about trusting you to see your friends. Sorting out family and school disagreements is all about compromising. If you show willing your parents are bound to give your friends a second chance. ★

❝No one likes the real me.❞

Fitting in at school can be hard. Everyone always looks trendy, cool and happy, while you are left to feel the odd one out every time. If you feel that no one can possibly like the real you, ask yourself how you know that for sure. In fact, only superficial people will refuse to be friends if you don't look cool, and you don't really want friends like that anyway, do you?

Real friends are people who accept you warts and all. They like you because of who you are, not because of what you wear and who you hang out with. Realising this and acting upon it is something that most of us have to go through at some point in our lives. You can't spend your whole life pretending to be something you're not, because it will make you even more unhappy and more depressed. People always respect and like individuals who have the courage to stick up for themselves. ★

6 She boasts about her school work. 9

As I've already said, school work isn't competitive, but that doesn't stop some people trying to make you feel terrible for not doing as well as them. If you have school mates like this, ask yourself why they do it. People who draw attention to themselves with boasts and lies do so because they are insecure. A boastful classmate obviously thinks no one knows she is good at her work. By boasting she is trying to boost her public image. It may seem like a bizarre way to get people to notice you, but imagine how desperate such people must be. However, it's not easy to live with a school friend like this. If I were you, I'd sit down and have a talk with her. Point out that you like her without all her boasts, and that she doesn't need to try so hard to get people's attention. With a few words of encouragement and support you can help her to break this habit. ★

CHAPTER SIX

SEX

WOW!

Sex' is a word guaranteed to cause copious amounts of giggles and sniggers. It's also a word that has generated the most amount of rubbish ever! Just take a look at this list.

'It's unhealthy to be a virgin.'
'You can't get pregnant the first time you have sex.'
'He says it's dangerous for boys not to have sex once they get an erection.'
'Everyone's doing it.'

These are just some of the most common myths I hear regarding sex. All of the above, are a load of rubbish and if anyone tries these on you, tell them to get lost. Sex is a personal issue, not a competition or something to be gossiped about with your friends.

Of course, even though sex is a natural thing it still freaks the majority of us out. We can't help but think everyone is better at it than us, everyone knows just what to do and everyone is an expert. But none of us are born with a natural talent for sex. It takes a combination of time and experimentation with the right person to get sex just right. Please note that this is not a good excuse to jump into bed with just anyone! If anything, sex with the wrong person can be a truly horrible experience. And while sex can be an okay experience with someone you don't love, it really is a million times better with someone you truly care about.

So do yourself a favour and make sure you know all there is to know about sex before you make a decision about it. To be informed is to be empowered. Sure sex is great, exciting and fun. But it's also scary, and even life-threatening, if you don't take the right precautions.

GETTING TO GRIPS

WITH SEX

❝I'm sixteen and still a virgin.❞

The age of consent is 16 years old. This basically means that it is illegal for any male to have sex with a girl who is under 16 years old (17 years old in Northern Ireland). This is by no means a marker for losing your virginity. It's only a legal device to protect young girls. Being 16 and having sex are completely unrelated. You have a right to say no, whatever your age. You should not have sex until you are responsible, ready and sure of your partner. This means making sure you use contraception, practising safer sex (this means using a condom) and not letting anyone pressurise you into it. If in any doubt, don't do it. Remember, sex is an easy act but living with the consequences isn't. If you haven't protected yourself, or have let yourself be pushed into it, the chances are you're going to feel terrible the next day.

By the way, even though a girl cannot be prosecuted for unlawful sex with a boy who is under 16 years old, in certain extreme cases, she can be prosecuted for indecent assault. ★

⑥I want a baby.⑨

Having a child is not a solution to any problem. It won't make you feel happy, fulfilled and loved, if you don't feel these things already. Having a child is a huge responsibility and will only make your life more difficult. Some girls consider tricking their boyfriend into being a father, but this is not only irresponsible, it's also totally unfair. The implications of such a deception are horrendous both financially (he'll have to pay child support for the rest of his life) and emotionally. If you are considering this, ask yourself how you'll cope with nowhere to live and no money. If this doesn't convince you, then think about the child. Doesn't he or she deserve to have the best chance in the world? What kind of life can you offer it? If you're really desperate for children don't rush into having one, there are plenty of other things you can do. Get involved with a local playgroup or children's charity in your area. (You can get details from your local library.)

★

❝What is the pill and how does it work?❞

The pill is dose of hormones that a girl swallows. There are over thirty different brands of the pill, all a bit different and all containing a different amount of chemical hormones. The combined pill contains two artificial hormones - oestrogen and progestogen. These hormones prevent an egg from ripening and from being released from an ovary. If no egg is released, there's absolutely no chance of a girl getting pregnant.

The pill is only available on prescription from your GP or clinic as it is not suitable for everyone. Though it is 98% reliable against pregnancy, it is no protection against AIDS or sexually transmitted diseases. This is why you should always use a condom as well. ★

❝My boyfriend doesn't like using condoms.❞

This is one of the worst excuses ever for not using contraception. Many boys say that having sex with a condom isn't 'real' or 'the same' but this is a load of rubbish! Condoms are made of very thin rubber and make very little difference to the sensation of having sex.

Even if you're using the pill as a method of contraception it is also worth using a condom for added protection against getting pregnant. (With careful use, the condom is 98% effective.) But besides preventing an unwanted pregnancy, condoms are a barrier method of contraception. They are the ONLY thing which will protect you from HIV - the virus which can lead to AIDS, and they also help to protect you from other sexually transmitted diseases.

Bearing all this in mind, if a boy refuses to wear a condom then you need to consider if he really does care about you. AIDS will kill you. If this boy isn't going to be responsible enough to protect himself and you, then the chances are he doesn't have your best interests at heart and you shouldn't be having sex with him.

Condoms can be bought in any chemist and are available free at any Family Planning Clinic. Make sure you always check the 'use by' date and look to see if the packet bears a British kitemark symbol. (This symbol shows it has been tested to British standards). ★

❝I can't say no to sex.❞

Some girls sleep with a lot of boys, some girls don't. Whatever you do, it's your choice, and yours alone. Ignore all those idiots who shout 'slag' or 'easy lay' at girls who have slept with a few guys. There is no such thing as a 'slag' or 'being easy'. These are abusive and sexist terms which mean nothing. Girls are allowed to be as sexual as boys, no matter what some ignorant people think.

However, if you are someone who has sex with a lot of people and regret it, you may need to question why you do it. It doesn't mean you're abnormal, but it could mean you have low self-esteem. Take 16 year-old Sarah - she wrote to me saying she could never say no to boys when they asked her to sleep with them. Was it because she liked them so much or because she enjoyed having sex? Actually it was for neither of these reasons. She felt that if she didn't say yes to their demands she'd lose them and be alone again. The only trouble was, even when she slept with them, she still lost them.

The only way round a problem like this is to never give in to a boy's demands over sex. It doesn't matter how many times you've had sex before or if you are a virgin. If you don't want to have sex then don't do it. Your body is yours and yours alone. No one has a right to dictate what you should and shouldn't do with it. The plain truth is that if a boy is pressurising you to have sex, he doesn't have your best interests at heart.

Having sex to keep a boy interested, or to prove you are attractive will never work. Improving your self-esteem will. Not only will it empower you to make choices that are right for you, but it will also help you to feel better about your self and your body. ★

⑥ Everyone knows about oral sex apart from me...⑨

It's more likely that everyone pretends they know about it when really they don't! Oral sex means using your mouth on your partner's sex organs. When oral sex is performed on a girl it's called cunnilingus and when it is performed on a boy it is called fellatio. There are a couple of things you should remember about oral sex. One is if that if you aren't absolutely 100% sure that your partner doesn't have HIV (the virus which leads to AIDS), you should use a condom for oral sex, as the virus is carried in semen. Contrary to popular myth, there is absolutely no way you can get pregnant from oral sex even if you do swallow sperm. ★

Is it normal to bleed when you have sex for the first time?

Lots of girls bleed when they have sex for the first time. this is because the vagina is covered by a thin membrane of skin called the hymen. The hymen partly covers the entrance to your vagina. It used to be thought this was the only way you could tell if a girl was a virgin or not. However, it can be broken very easily through sport or the use of tampons, so it is no indication of virginity at all! If it does break during sex it can cause a certain amount of bleeding but it is nothing to worry about. ★

How can I find out what happens during an orgasm?

WOW!

Thanks to TV and films, orgasms have quite a reputation to live up to! Basically, an orgasm follows a similar pattern for both girls and boys, although the feelings and sensation often differ, both from person to person and from time to time.

First of all there is the arousal stage. This is when our bodies start to feel ready for sex. Sexual excitement then builds up, and at the peak, the sex organs contract in a series of spasms, and a feeling of release and pleasure flows through out the body. Boys have an obvious physical sign, ejaculation. But girls don't, and it's often less easy for girls to tell whether or not they've had an orgasm. Some women describe the feeling as fireworks going off, others are less dramatic about it. The truth is that all women respond differently and each orgasm can vary in intensity. ★

What is foreplay?

Foreplay is what happens before penetration. This includes kissing, hugging, stroking and heavy petting, and can also involve oral sex too. Foreplay is very important because it prepares the vagina for penetration. When you get aroused, the vagina produces a natural lubricant which makes it easier for the penis to enter.

Foreplay won't make you pregnant as long as you're careful. But if your boyfriend touches his penis then your vagina, you are at risk. Always make sure your boyfriend wears a condom as soon as he has an erection. ★

How do you put on a condom?

Condoms come in a packet and are rolled up. To use one, take it out of the packet and squeeze the closed end to expel any air that might be lurking there (this is the end the semen collects in). Carefully unroll it onto an erect penis. It may be a bit awkward the first few times you try to put one on, but with a bit of practice it can be done in a matter of seconds. After sex, make sure the condom doesn't slip off when your boyfriend withdraws.

Condoms now come in a variety of different textures, colours, flavours - but as long as they have a kitemark on the packet and haven't passed their sell by date they are fine to use. ★

⑤What's the morning after pill?⑨

★If you have had sex without using contraception, you can use the 'morning after' pill (also known as the post-coital pill). This can only be prescribed by a doctor and must be taken within 72 hours of having sex. It is taken in the form of two pills, which must be taken 12 hours apart. If you are sick within the first hour of taking either of these two pills you must go back to the doctor. This is an emergency method only - not a form of contraception, as it cannot be used every time you have sex.

⑤I think I'm pregnant!⑨

The first thing you must do is pay a visit to your doctor, a Family Planning Clinic or a Brook Advisory Centre. They will be able to give you a free pregnancy test to find out if you are definitely pregnant or not. If you are, they can then advise you on your next step. This is the stage where you will have to tell your parents, mainly because you will not be able to cope on your own. You can choose to terminate your pregnancy by having an abortion, but you'll need to make this decision pretty soon, as abortions have to be carried out as early in pregnancy as possible. Very few doctors now perform an abortion after 20 weeks, as the later the abortion, the more difficult, risky and unpleasant it is. Whatever you decide, don't try to go through this alone. You need to surround yourself with people who care about you so you can get through this traumatic time. ★

Lies, Myths and the truth about Sex

❝I'm worried that I'm frigid.❞

Girls who don't want to have sex are often accused of being frigid. This is yet another form of sexual pressure. There is no medical condition called frigidity - it doesn't exist. It's just a made up term that boys use as an excuse when a girl says no.

If you do feel yourself freezing, tensing up or panicking when a boy tries to have sex with you, it's not because you're rubbish at sex. It's probably because you don't really want to do it!

Sex is supposed to be fun - not something to get upset about. If you can't relax, it could also be that your partner's not right for you. ★

How often should you have sex?

There are no set rules when it comes to sex. Unfortunately, some people feel that once they have sex there is no going back to plain old kissing. But the fact is, you can do whatever you want, whenever you want. Films and TV would have us believe that passionate sex goes on and on, and once you've found the real thing you just can't keep your hands off each other. While this can be true for a short while, it's never long lasting.

As long as you have sex when you want it, not when you feel you should have it, everything will be fine. Ignore the friends who tell you they have it all the time. Either they are being competitive (and sex isn't something to be competitive about) or they are lying. Remember, it's a case of different strokes for different folks. Some people have sex once a day, others once a month. It doesn't really matter as long as both you and your partner are happy with the arrangement. ★

Does sex lead to love?

Contrary to popular belief, sex and love don't always come together. It's very possible to love someone deeply and yet not have sex with them. Likewise many people have sex with people they don't love.

Don't have sex in the hope it will make someone fall in love with you - it won't. Love is about respect, communication and friendship on a deeper level, while sex is more of a physical need. It is possible to have enjoyable sex without love, but sex is a million times better with someone you do love. ★

⑤Is masturbation bad for you?⑨

Masturbation means giving yourself sexual pleasure, or literally making love to yourself. It doesn't make you blind, infertile, bad at sex or anything like that. Some people feel it's disgusting because they view masturbation as a selfish pleasure. Others say it's only for people who are single. But in fact, the majority of the population masturbates in some form or another.

Masturbation is actually a perfectly normal and natural way to learn about your body. Most boys masturbate by rubbing their penis, while girls usually masturbate by rubbing their clitoris. (This is the main organ for female sexual pleasure and is located at the top of the outer lips of your vagina.) There is no 'should' about masturbation, if you don't like the sound of it, you don't have to do it. ★

⑤Is withdrawal a method of contraception?⑨

Withdrawal is when a boy takes his penis out of your vagina just before ejaculation. It is a thoroughly unreliable method of contraception because semen can actually leak from the penis before a boy withdraws. While we're talking about myths, remember that all the following are complete lies too:

You can't get pregnant if you have sex for the first time.
Sex standing up is a method of contraception.
You can re-use a condom.
It's unhealthy for boys not to have sex.
Boys are more highly sexed than girls.
Boys can tell if you're a virgin.
The pill will protect you from AIDS.
Having sex during your period is a method of contraception.
Oral sex can make you pregnant.
Sex with a condom makes it less pleasurable.

Sexual health

ʕWhat is AIDS?ʔ

AIDS stands for Acquired Immune Deficiency Syndrome. 'Acquired' means that it is an illness you can catch, not one you're born with. 'Immune Deficiency' means that your body is unable to defend itself against infections and illnesses. And 'Syndrome' refers to a group of illnesses. At the moment, the virus HIV and about 25 different diseases are used to identify AIDS. AIDS is a fatal disease and there is no cure. Both heterosexuals (people who are attracted to the opposite sex) and homosexuals (both men and women who are attracted to members of their own sex) are at risk of catching AIDS, so don't think that it can't happen to you.

AIDS develops after a person has been infected with HIV (Human Immunodeficiency Virus). This is the virus which attacks and destroys your body's defence system (immune system). There is a difference between having HIV and AIDS. HIV can stay in the blood stream for up to ten years without any sign of AIDS. However, during this time people with HIV can transmit this virus to other people. This doesn't mean you can catch it from touching someone, or drinking from a cup or sitting on a toilet seat, as the HIV virus can't live outside the body. To get inside the body it has to be passed through blood or body fluids, such as sperm. This is why unprotected sex (sex without a condom) is so dangerous. As is sharing needles if you are a drug addict. To help protect yourself, limit your sexual partners and always use a condom. ★

‘I can't get over having an abortion.’

Any person that says an abortion is an easy decision doesn't know what they're talking about. Abortion is never an easy choice to make. If you've had an abortion and are suffering, you have to believe that you are not being punished. An abortion is a personal decision based on what is right for you, and no one has a right to say this is wrong. The mixed emotions a woman experiences after an abortion are completely natural and normal. Most women who have had an abortion feel a mixture of relief, anger, guilt and misery. If you feel like this and can't get over what has happened, contact a Brook Advisory Centre. Brook offers post-abortion counselling for anyone who needs it. The service is completely confidential and sympathetic. ★

‘What do I do if I think I have a sexually transmitted disease?’

If you suspect that you have a sexually transmitted disease (sometimes known as an STD or VD) it is important to get medical help quickly. Possible signs include discharge and/or itchiness, pain when you urinate and spots or warts on your vagina. If you think you have something wrong, you need to go to your nearest Special Clinic (also known as a VD clinic or Genito-Urinary Clinic) details of which will be in your local directory under S, V or G. Your doctor cannot treat you herself because specialist facilities are needed to diagnose STDs. You don't need a letter from your GP to be referred, you can just turn up. Diagnosis and treatment are confidential and free. ★

⟨What is a smear test?⟩

A smear test checks for any early changes in your cervix which could later lead to cancer. Doctors recommend you have your first test one year after becoming sexually active, then one every three years.

The test is often performed by a nurse or doctor who will place a metal or plastic instrument (called a speculum) into your vagina so she can look at the cervix. A small scraping or smear is then taken from the surface of the cervix with a tiny wooden spatula. The smear is then taken to a laboratory to be examined. The test is painless and very quick. It is very important to have this test if you are having sex on a regular basis. If you still aren't convinced that you should have one, it may reassure you to know that pre-cancerous conditions are 100% curable if you catch them in time to treat them. ★

⟨I think I've got thrush.⟩

Thrush is also known as Candida. It is a very common illness and is caused by a yeast fungus living in the vagina. Usually this fungus is kept under control but when you're ill or feeling run-down it can become out of control. Symptoms include a thick discharge, terrible itching, and pain when you pass urine. It isn't usually sexually transmitted but you can pass it on to your boyfriend during sex if you don't use a condom. You can avoid thrush by washing your vagina every day and always wearing clean cotton knickers. Your GP can prescribe pessaries (special vaginal tablets) that will clear it up as soon as possible, or you can buy them over the counter at a chemist's. ★

CHAPTER SEVEN

SEX-UALITY

Sexuality is a personal thing. Whether you're gay, straight, bisexual or completely non-sexual, it's up to you and you alone. Telling people what your sexual preference is, is also up to you. If you're gay and want to keep it a secret don't let other people pressurise you into coming out. If you think you might fancy girls and boys - so what? It's your life and as long as you don't hurt anyone it's up to you what you do with it.

Unfortunately, homophobia is still rife. Some people say they hate gays because it's 'unnatural' to fall in love with someone of the same sex. This is a load of rubbish. Nobody can help who they fall in love with, it's often a combination of different factors. It's actually hating someone just because they are different which is unnatural and abnormal.

No one knows why some people are gay and others aren't, but the fact is, people can't make you gay and neither can books or films. There are some hysterical people who think just talking about it persuades people to be gay but this isn't true. If you are worried about your sexuality don't hide your true feelings away. Coming to terms with who you are is hard, and it's often even worse if you just lock up all your true feelings and try to be something you're not.

If you can't talk to friends and family about your worries, there are a number of organisations who can and will help. (You'll find their names and addresses at the back of this book.) They won't persuade you that you're gay, straight or anything else for that matter. They'll just help you to come to terms with your mixed feelings. After all, it isn't easy being gay in a culture that's geared so strongly towards being straight, but realising that you're not alone and that there are people who can help, makes life a hundred times easier.

Being gay

The fear that you might be homosexual is one of the most common teenage fears. It may help to realise that although most of us end up with a definite preference, very few people are 100% heterosexual or homosexual. This doesn't mean that the majority of us have physical relationships with both sexes but it does mean most of us are capable of feeling some kind of attraction to members of both sexes.

There is nothing strange or mysterious about being gay or straight. It is just a label, like being tall, short, English or French. How you choose to define yourself is up to you, and if you don't want to tell anyone who you are, then that's up to you too. Whether you love men or women or both isn't important. What is important, is your ability to give and accept love.

I fancy girls. Am I gay ?

Many of us go through a time in our lives when we're not sure who we are. One minute we're sure we fancy a guy in our class, only to find an hour later we are attracted to a girl we know. While some people are sure from a very early age that they are gay, the majority of us aren't that certain. Putting a label on yourself when you're not sure is pointless. In time, your sexual identity will become clearer and you'll know for definite if it's girls, boys or both that you fancy. Until then, don't rush to label yourself as anything. And remember, just because you fancy girls, it doesn't mean you're gay. Admiring someone we find attractive, no matter what their sex, is a sign of a well-rounded person. ★

❝I'm gay and I hate it!❞

The feelings you are going through are completely normal, as anyone who has ever 'come out' will tell you. Discovering that you're gay isn't easy - mainly because society is currently so homophobic it can be very hard to tell others. However, just because you're gay it doesn't mean you're destined for a life of loneliness. The image of the lonely gay person has no basis in reality. Just like heterosexuals the majority of gay people have partners who share their lives.

If you feel like this, it would really help you to talk to someone in a similar position so that you can see that you're not alone. The Lesbian and Gay Switchboard run a 24 hour service for anyone who needs to talk. Don't rush into coming out until you have come to terms with your feelings. Sexual identity is a personal thing. Take your time and do it when you feel happier about who you are. Remember, you have nothing to feel bad about. Being gay is part of who you are, just as your height, weight and shoe size is part of you. ★

❝Am I bisexual?❞

Just because you fancy both men and women doesn't necessarily mean you are bisexual. Lots of people find members of the same sex attractive and even fantasize about them but are still straight. Finding other women attractive means as little or as much as you want it to.

Of course, some people are very sure that they are bisexual, and if you're one of these people then fine. No one is innately heterosexual or homosexual - we make choices based on how we feel and how strong our sexual urges are.

As long as you practice safe sex and are honest about yourself to your partner you won't be hurting anyone, least of all yourself. Of course, straight friends might be shocked and scared when you announce you have fallen for another girl but don't let this pressurise you into making a snap decision as to whether you are gay or straight. You may be one or you may be neither. As long as you're honest to yourself, you don't owe anyone an explanation. ★

❝I'm in love with a female teacher, does this mean I'm gay?❞

All you are doing is confusing admiration for love. Lots of people have role models of the same sex. It's important to have positive role models that give you some sort of idea of the kind of woman you want to be. This is why crushes on teachers are so common. It's comforting to find a woman who has the kind of life or is the kind of person you'd like to be one day. It's healthy to feel this way and doesn't mean you're strange, odd or weird in any way.

Don't take your feelings for a teacher to be a sure sign you're gay. If you are you'll know in time, but for the moment, don't be in such a rush to label yourself. Girls always have role models they feel they are in love with when they're growing up. These role models are important and significant parts of our lives. They can help us shape our future, decide what we want from relationships and guide us. But they are rarely anything more than that.

If you are worried that you may become obsessed with a female teacher, try to limit the amount of time you spend with her. Hang around with your friends instead of waiting around for her, and make sure you go out at weekends so you don't have time to think about her. This will help you to put your feelings into perspective and show you that all you have is an innocent friendship. ★

Coming Out

I'm gay

I won't say that coming out is easy, but I will say that coming out is easier than spending your whole life pretending to be something you're not. Of course, there are going to be people who don't understand, and these may include your parents. But you should never let other people's prejudices stop you from being true to yourself. After all being gay isn't an illness. It's an alternative to being straight, and don't let anyone ever tell you otherwise. Homophobia breeds on ignorance and stupidity and you should speak out against it. Yet, despite what some gay groups say, coming out is a personal issue and one which you should do only when you feel ready. If you are thinking of coming out you may find it helpful to talk to someone about it before you do anything. Both Lesbian and Gay Switchboard and London Friend offer such counselling help.

❝My parents won't speak to me now that I'm gay.❞

A bad reaction from your parents can have more to do with dashed hopes than the fact you're gay. After all, just because you've come out, it doesn't mean you've suddenly changed personality. You're still the same person you were before you said,

'I'm gay'. The only thing that has changed is their perception of you. Your parents' hopes of a wedding, grandchildren and everything that comes with marriage will have been destroyed. Don't immediately think they hate you for being gay, they don't. Parents have a habit of planning your future without your consent and find it hard to deal with when you turn round and point out you have a different view. Don't let parental guilt drive you to despair, talk to them and point out you are the same person you were before you announced you were gay. In time they will hopefully come round.

Here are some quotes from other teenagers who have come out.

☆ 'I was never sure if I was gay or not until I was about 17 years old. Then I started seeing this girl I met at a concert. I didn't know what to do because I knew how my parents felt about gay people, especially lesbians. In the end I 'confessed' to my best friend and she was brilliant. She gave me the courage to tell my parents. Sure they weren't thrilled, but two years later they are finally coming to terms with it.'

Yas (19)

☆ 'I am a 15 year-old gay boy. My friends had very prejudiced views about gays. They thought all gays had floppy wrists and lisps! They used to say other childish and hurtful comments like this but I came out all the same. They were shocked and surprised but very supportive. You see they never knew any gay people and I have made them see that their views were wrong. This is why you should tell people you're gay. It'll force them to change their views.'

Tom (15)

☆ 'My parents took the news very hard. My father wouldn't speak to me for months because he said I'd cheated him out of grandchildren. Then one day I got mad and said he was cheating me out of a life by not letting me be true to myself. Two days later he apologised and said he supported and loved me no matter who I was. Knowing that has changed my whole life.'

Donna (16)

cOpinG WiTh SomeOne CominG oUt

Being on the other side of coming out can be hard. If someone close to you has recently told you they are gay, or you suspect a friend may be gay, then really think before you say anything. Often, people choose the person they trust and care about most to come out to. Your reaction, therefore, is the one they will look to as an example of how others will react. There's nothing wrong with admitting you're shocked and need time to deal with it, but being mean and vicious is not only cruel, it could also ruin their life.

❝My mum's just announced she's a lesbian and I hate her for it. I'll be a laughing stock when everyone hears about this...❞

The first thing you must do is talk to your mum and let her explain why she came out. I'm sure she doesn't expect you to applaud her decision and carry on as if nothing had happened. If anything, she will have already thought about the very worries and fears you're going through now. Choosing to come out after all these years must have been a hard decision for her. Imagine having to hide your true feelings for years and years and never being able to tell anyone how you really feel. This is exactly how your mum must have felt.

I'd like you to meet...

WHAT?!!*

While this doesn't solve your own problems, it might help you to hate her less. What you need to realise is that your mother is no more a reflection of you than you are of her. If people choose to dislike you just because she's a lesbian then that's their problem not yours. ★

⑥I hate my best friend for saying she's gay.⑨

Ask yourself whether it's her you hate, or the idea that she's gay? The chances are it's the latter. All that has changed is your perception of her. Your best friend is still the same person she was before she said those three words to you. Remember, whatever she is, it's no one else's business but her own. She has chosen to tell you because she trusts you. Don't betray her friendship by running away. It's okay to feel awkward or funny about it. No one expects you to accept it straight away. Just talk to her and see what she has to say. If you're true friends you'll find a way to work it out. ★

the Dating game

Same-sex relationships are as difficult to cope with as straight ones. Fear of rejection, worries about being single, and heartbreak are all the same whether you're dating a boy or a girl. However, you can help yourself by being sure of what you're doing, always using a condom and not being promiscuous. ★

❝I told my girlfriend I thought I was straight. Now I realise I was wrong but she won't go back out with me!❞

I think you're really under-estimating how much you hurt your girlfriend and what she went through to get over you. Break-ups are very painful things, and long after you've forgiven the person who caused the split, you can still remember what you went through. It isn't easy dealing with a break-up especially if the person you're dating isn't sure of their sexuality. Once you know how much someone can hurt you, the thought of doing it all over again isn't very tempting. If you've made your position clear and she knows how you feel, then the only thing you can do is give her time. ★

⁶My friends don't like my girlfriend.⁹

You're never going to be able to please everybody all of the time so your best bet is to please yourself. It doesn't really matter if your friends like your girlfriend or not, because they're not the ones dating her, you are. Looking at their motives may help you to see why they dislike her. Is it because she is the first girl you've ever gone out with? If so, maybe their dislike has more to do with their uneasiness about your homosexuality. If this is the case, then talk to them about your worries. Above all, trust your own instincts. If you love your girlfriend, then keep going out with her. Leaving her just because your friends put pressure on you will only cause you to hate yourself and hate them. Tell them that while you respect their opinion, you don't agree with it. ★

Chapter eight

LIVING WITH YOURSELF

Being yourself can be hard. Apart from the ups and downs of school life, and the trials and tribulations of relationships and friendships, actually having to put up with yourself can be a miserable experience if you have no self-esteem.

Of course, there are times when we all look in the mirror and think, 'Yuk! I hate myself!', but if you do this every day and let it get you down, then you need to change your attitude to life. Likewise, if you're someone who always says mean things and then feels guilty or can't be nice to anyone, then the chances are you're very unhappy.

Of course, we can't expect to be happy every moment of our lives, but if you never feel happy, and always feel depressed or even suicidal, then it's time to ask for help.

Growing-up is hard and learning to come to terms with the parts of us we can't change is harder still. Some people never manage to do it and spend their whole lives wishing they were someone else. Believing that if they were thinner or smaller or taller or richer or smarter... they would be happier. But the key to happiness is your attitude and the way you look at things. So what, if you're spotty, overweight and shy? So are a lot of other people. And what's more, you won't feel like this forever. You can become anything and do anything you want. All you have to do is have a bit of faith in yourself. So what, if your teacher thinks you'll never amount to much? Or you've never had a boyfriend? Or your parents don't encourage you? As long as you've got a mind of your own, you've got the capacity to forge ahead and do whatever you want.

The hardest part of life is learning to deal with all your private fears and insecurities. The parts of you that you never dare tell anyone because you're sure they won't understand. Things like death, self-image, self-abuse and suicide. But keeping these anxieties locked up is even scarier, because it only makes them worse. It's rather like being stuck in a long dark tunnel, and being too scared to call out. The longer you stay silent, the more lost and scared you're going to get. Calling out is the only chance you have of finding the light at the end of the tunnel.

After all, some secrets aren't meant to be kept. If you are hurting yourself or someone is hurting you, then you have to ask for help. Some problems can't be solved on their own and you owe it to yourself to get help.

Loving your self warts and all

It's hard not to agonise over your body when every time you turn on the TV, open a magazine, or watch a film, there are images of skinny women with extra long legs, perfect breasts and shiny hair wandering in front of your eyes. And it's hard not to become obsessed with what you eat when everyone from your mother to your friends seems to be on a diet. When boys are 'allowed' to stuff their faces and you 'have to' suck on a lettuce leaf. When adverts for Diet Pepsi are specifically aimed at women while Pepsi Max (also Diet Pepsi) are aimed at boys. But surely women are supposed to diet, aren't they? While men aren't?

The fact is there's a huge diet culture in the Western world aimed specifically at women. We're made to feel conscious of our bodies from an early age and encouraged to watch what we eat, because if we're not slim then we're supposedly not attractive. Yet, we're not all born to look like supermodels. We all come in different shapes and sizes, with different hip measurements and different body weights. Not all of us have to have 'manageable, shiny hair' that bounces when we walk. Or clear, perfect skin that 'glows with health'.

A 'normal' woman has hair that doesn't go right some mornings, gets spots when she's stressed out and stuffs her face with chocolate when she wants to. She is a real person, not some advertisement for a 'perfect' woman. No one is ever 100% happy with the way they look but as long as you feel about 80% happy then you're on the right track. If you think you're scoring about 20% then it's time to reassess your attitude to yourself.

Having a good body image is important because it makes up a vital part of our self-confidence and esteem. If we hate the way we look then we don't project ourselves in a positive way to people we meet. If we think we're ugly, unattractive and disgusting, then if anyone is ever nice to us we think there must be something wrong with them.

After all, what is there to like? If they were okay people then they wouldn't be talking to us!

If you don't like yourself, you can't expect anyone else to like you back. Learning to respect yourself, warts and all, is a way of saying, 'Hey, look! I'm a good person. I'm worth knowing'. You don't have to make excuses for yourself or what you look like. You are who you are, and if people can't accept you for that, then that's their loss not yours.

❝I'm too fat.❞

The most important thing to do is to find out for sure if you are overweight or not. Don't bother with those silly charts or weighing scales at home. Go to your GP and let her tell you for sure whether you need to lose weight or not. If you do, she will give you a diet sheet that will help you to eat properly.

If you are determined to lose weight anyway, ask yourself why. Is it because you'll feel better and healthier? If this is the case taking up exercise will help just as much and be more enjoyable. Or is it because you think it will improve your life or get you a boyfriend? If you're hoping that losing weight will be a magical cure for all the things you're unhappy about in your life, then you could well be in for a surprise. Weight gain or loss is just that and nothing else. It doesn't have the power to make your life perfect. Of course, it could improve your self-confidence and make you more assertive, but it won't make your life wonderful. Take a look at what makes you unhappy and then seriously ask yourself if this is related to your weight.

Battling with weight is a problem for many people, but if you are too obsessed with dieting it can become a bigger problem than losing weight. For instance, are you so calorie obsessed that all you think about is what you eat? Is food on your mind all the time? Do you not eat and then look at pictures of food in magazines? If this sounds like you, then you need to reassess your attitude to food. Being overweight may not be healthy but it's better than yo-yo dieting and making yourself depressed and miserable for the rest of your life.

If you do decide to diet, then make sure you do it properly and don't crash diet. Crash dieting only makes you put on MORE weight in the end! This is because not eating puts your body in starvation mode, it slows down your metabolism (the rate at which you use up food) and stops you losing weight. Then when you do start eating again, your body clings onto everything you eat and stores it up as fat, so you can't lose weight. You are much better off learning how to eat healthily. Not only will this last for the rest of your life but it will also stop you becoming obsessed with food. This means cutting out refined foods and eating lots of fresh fruits and vegetables, grilling or baking your food instead of frying it, and cutting down on chips, crisps, chocolates and fizzy drinks. Don't cut out so much of your favourite things that you start craving them. Be sensible and don't over do it. ★

𝔖I'm too thin!𝔖

While thin girls are often the envy of their friends, being skinny and unable to put on weight can be a huge problem for some. If you are naturally thin, then exercising could help you a great deal. Muscles can add curves to your body and make you feel better about yourself.

If you think you are seriously underweight don't just stuff your body full of sugary snacks, it's very important to make sure you eat proper nutritious food. Try and keep a diary of all the food you eat in a week and then go along and see your GP. She can tell you for sure if you need to go on a high calorie diet or not.

If you are thin, it doesn't mean you can't be attractive. Lots of thin women are seen as being just as sexy as curvaceous ones. Don't pin all your hopes on getting a voluptuous figure when the chances of it happening are remote. Be realistic about your body shape. Just as most larger women will never be waif-like, most thin girls will never be voluptuous. Telling yourself you can never be happy the way you are is just the same as giving up. We are what we are and we have to learn to accept that and make the best of ourselves. ★

⟨Am I anorexic?⟩

Teenage girls need to consume at least 2000 calories a day in order to sustain the necessary changes the body undertakes during puberty. Very low calorie diets interfere with this process and can even stop your growth all together. If you are starving yourself, or eating less than 1000 calories a day (about one meal), then you are starving your body of energy, nutrients and vital vitamins and minerals. Physical symptoms will include fainting, nausea, depression, bad skin, tiredness and lethargy.

Anorexia Nervosa is a disease which is about more than excessive dieting. The sufferer can starve herself to the point of death without realising that she is thin. An anorexic will always look at herself in the mirror and think she is fat, no matter how thin she is. Anorexia is in fact, a cry for help and the sufferer needs professional care. It's self-destructive, and a terrible way to try to control a life you don't understand. If you think you are anorexic, or know someone who needs help, contact the Eating Disorders Association. (You'll find their address at the back of this book) ★

⟨I think I am bulimic.⟩

Bulimia is an eating disorder just as serious as anorexia. It is also known as the binge/purge syndrome. This basically means that girls who are bulimic eat, then make themselves sick, in order to control their weight. Some girls don't eat for days, then consume huge amounts of calories in a very short time, only to vomit it all up. Like anorexia, this disorder destroys your vital organs and state of mind. If you think you have this disorder you need to get help to control it before it starts to control you. Contact the Eating Disorders Association or your GP. ★

Ab^uSe

Abuse comes in lots of different forms. We can be abused sexually, mentally or physically by others, while we can also abuse ourselves. Self-abuse includes addictions, like drink and drugs, and self-injury.

Abuse has its roots in lots of different things but one thing is for sure, you don't have to put up with it. Whether you do it to yourself or others do it to you, put a stop to it now by asking for help. Abuse can be overcome with help and support.

❝I have a problem with drugs and drink.❞

Addiction to drink and drugs is more common than you probably think. If you are addicted to these things it doesn't mean you are

a terrible person. Many people turn to drink and drugs as a way out of a deeper problem. Most want to feel better about life and about themselves and hope that an artificial 'high' will do it for them. But what they don't realise is that drugs and drinks are actually depressants. The high is only temporary. When you come down you'll feel worse than you did before, leading you to crave more drink or drugs and leading you into a vicious circle. If you take substances instead of learning to cope with the real pressures you will never overcome your problems. In fact, the drugs and drink will only perpetuate into a downward spiral and make all your problems a hundred times worse.

While it's not easy to stop abusing alcohol and drugs it can be done. Keeping away from temptation is a start. Friends who encourage you to take drink and drugs aren't real friends. Real friends want you to be yourself and be well. If you make a decision to stop, take one day at a time, and if you slip up, don't give up. Ask your friends and family to help and be patient with yourself. Everyone has problems and we all find them hard to deal with. In saying no to harmful substances, you are taking control of your life and taking a step towards dealing with what upset you. ★

❝I cut myself.❞

Self-injury is a term which can be used for a variety of things which we do to ourselves to harm us. It is a broad term to describe what happens when we turn on ourselves and inflict harm on our body. It includes things like scratching, cutting, slashing and biting ourselves. It is a direct result of anger and frustration and is often used as a way of coping and dealing with despair. If you are attacking yourself in this way you need to ask for help. The Bristol Crisis Service For Women specialise in helping women who hurt themselves (their address is at the back of this book). ★

❝I think I am being sexually abused.❞

Sexual abuse occurs when an adult or older person touches or uses a young person in a sexual way. It's always wrong because your body is yours and yours alone. No one - no matter who they are - has the right to touch it, abuse it or hurt you in any way.

Incest is when the abuser is part of the immediate family. It is the ultimate betrayal, and has deeply traumatic affects which can last for years after the abuse has stopped. Many victims say that sexual abuse can have both physical and psychological affects on you. What's more, because it's such a taboo subject, victims often feel they are alone. In fact, figures now show that it is more widespread than anyone previously thought. If it is happening to you, you must seek help. Sexual abuse is NEVER the victim's fault. No one will blame you and people will believe you. If you can't turn to someone you know, contact Childline, your local social services, a teacher, a friend's parent or Rape Crisis. You owe it to yourself to protect your life. ★

death

Death is one of the last taboo subjects in our society. People don't like talking about it, which makes life for bereaved people extremely hard. Most people are afraid of death, but it's a natural part of life and inevitable to us all. For this very reason it is useless to waste time worrying about it and despairing over it. Having said that, losing someone you love is the most distressing part of life. But only people who refuse to love others can escape this and who wants to go through life without love?

❛I can't get over her death.❜

A sad fact of life is that we sometimes have to face situations of grief and loss. But it is through these that we learn to deal with circumstances we do not like but cannot change.

Losing someone you love is probably the most painful and distressing thing you will ever have to go through. Grieving is long and complicated, and there is no way you can rush it or refuse to go through it. The actual bereavement process has four main stages - shock, anger, depression and acceptance - each of which are distressing, but can be helped by talking about it with a person who cares and understands what you're going through. If there is no family member you can turn to, an outside counsellor can help.

The best and truest advice I can give you (and it sounds pretty lame) is that time is a great healer. Loss does become more bearable as time passes, and the pain, though it may never completely go away, does lessen and become easier to live with. ★

❛I'm afraid of dying!❜

Death is an inevitable part of our lives and therefore, we can't live without confronting it. However, because it is completely unavoidable, it's a waste of time to let it ruin your life. Worrying over where and when you're going to die, and about losing the people you love, achieves nothing. All it does is stop you from enjoying the present and making the most of being alive! I think you'll be surprised to know just how common your fears about death are. Lots of people worry so much about death that they become too afraid to enjoy life. Don't let your fears take over your life this way, if you talk to your parents you'll see they have probably gone through exactly the same anxieties as you. The only difference is that they have rationalised their fears and learnt to live in the present, not the future. Also, talking to them may help you to see death from a different perspective, one that isn't so scary. Remember, though death comes to us all, it's not something to become depressed about as it's out of our control. People are living longer every day, and you and most of the people you know could very well live to be 100 years old. ★

❝My friends are scared of me because I tried to kill myself.❞

People are often very scared by what they don't understand. Your suicide attempt was probably the first time your friends came close to seeing someone they cared about nearly die. It has no doubt frightened them and caused them to distance themselves from you. You have to realise they are not frightened of you but of what you tried to do. They may also be angry at you. I know this is irrational but people are often angry when someone they love comes close to death (for whatever reason). What you have to do is talk to them and show them you are still the same person you were before you tried to kill yourself. You can also point out that you are proof a troubled person should talk about their problems not bottle them up. ★

❝I want to kill myself.❞

Suicide is never an option. Apart from destroying your life it will also destroy the lives of those closest to you. There is NO problem that can't be worked out - as long as you ask for help. If you feel at all suicidal please don't give up on life, as there are a number of places and people that can and will help you come to terms with the pressure you're under. Both the Samaritans and Childline are on hand 24 hours a day, 365 days a year, and your GP can also refer you on to someone who can help. Talking through your problems with someone who understands is more helpful than you think. All worries are all things that can be worked through. They are not things to throw your life away over. Whatever you do, don't suffer alone. Seek help now. ★

❝I feel to blame for my boyfriend's suicide.❞

Your boyfriend must have been very depressed long before you went out with him. People just don't kill themselves on the spur of the moment. You are no more responsible for his suicide than his parents, his teachers or anyone else for that matter.

People who kill themselves do so out of desperation, frustration and an inability to see a way out of their present situation, not because they had a fight with a friend, or were annoyed with their girlfriend or boyfriend. More often than not it is a desperate bid for escape from a life they can't deal with. Sadly, such a death leaves everyone who is bereaved by it distressed and guilt-ridden, no matter how vaguely they knew the dead person. This is because there is always a feeling that a suicide could have been prevented.

In time, everything will work out but in the meantime you need to talk to someone who can help you to deal with your mixed emotions. CRUSE offers such confidential counselling to all bereaved young people. ★

❝I want to die too because I can't cope with their death.❞

Grief is a very complicated process. Losing someone you love is a deeply traumatic experience and often many people feel the only solution to their pain is to die too. But if you don't believe your life is important then think again. If you were to end your life now, think of all the things you'd be missing out on and of all you could achieve. Not only that but imagine putting your mother and friends through the same grief and suffering you're going through now. Would you really wish that on them?

If at any time you feel close to killing yourself, please tell someone. If you can't tell a friend or relative then try the Samaritans or Cruse (who specialise in bereavement counselling). ★

The real you

Who is the 'real' you? Are you the person who makes all your friends laugh, listens to all their problems and likes to go out? Or are you the person who cries themselves to sleep, worries they'll never amount to much and wonders if they really have any friends?
The chances are you're a combination of both.

We're all a complete mish-mash of confidence and insecurity. We all stand in a crowd and imagine everyone else is having a better time than us. We all wonder if we're boring or ugly or annoying. And we all sometimes wonder why anyone bothers to have anything to do with us. At the end of the day we're only human. We aren't perfect beings who are good all the time, never have a bad thought and never make a mistake.
As long as we are good to ourselves and the people we come into contact with, that's all we can ask for. Searching for perfection is a waste of time and effort. Making the most of what you've got, isn't.
If it means brushing your hair, smiling when you meet someone and saying yes when everyone else says no - then do it. After all, accepting who you are and what you are and capitalising on it is what life is all about.

❝I am depressed all the time.❞

Severe depression amongst teenagers is far more widespread than you might think. There are literally hundreds of girls across the country who feel as desperate as you, and hundreds more who have attempted suicide because they haven't had the courage to ask for help. In fact, MIND, the leading mental health organisation, estimates that one in eight teenagers suffer from depression. You have to realise that teenage depression is serious, which is why you must seek help as soon as possible for dealing with your frustration and despair.

The Samaritans offer confidential help and MIND produces an excellent leaflet on depression. ★

❝I'm too shy.❞

Shyness is the bane of many people's lives. If you're so shy that you can't bring yourself to talk to anyone, you have to realise two things. Firstly, no one is judging you or looking at you and waiting for you to do something wrong. They are all too worried that they might make a big mistake themselves to watch what you're doing. Secondly, if you don't make an effort with people, they won't make an effort with you. Don't stand around and merge in with the potted plants - smile when someone smiles at you. Try saying 'hello' even though you'd rather the ground just swallow you up and have a go at striking up conversation when you can. Terrifying, I know, but you can do it!

The trick is to ask people about themselves. Everyone likes to rattle on about themselves because we all find enquiries about ourselves flattering. Next remember and listen to what people say, instead of panicking when they are talking. This will enable you to think of the next question and help when you next see them again. And if all else fails, talk about TV, school, the weather - anything! ★

Often those of us who are shy are afraid to take a risk with people because we expect too much of ourselves. You don't have to be wildly funny, excessively clever or the life and soul of the party. You just have to be yourself. Don't prejudge people and they won't prejudge you. ★

❮I'm uncool!❯

Only superficial people will refuse to be friends if you don't look cool, and do you really want friends like that? You can't spend your whole life pretending to be something you're not, because it will make you even more unhappy and more depressed.

Don't worry about just being yourself. Don't be afraid to speak up when you don't want to do something, refuse to follow the crowd when you don't feel like it ,and stand your ground. If you start doing this, your real friends will admire you for yourself. After all, people always respect and like individuals who have the courage to stick up for themselves. ★

❮I'm ugly!❯

Take another look and don't be so hard on yourself! You may not be a supermodel - but then who is? I'm sure you don't hang out only with girls who are beautiful and likewise I'm sure you don't judge boys purely on their looks.

Often we are harder on ourselves then we are on other people. We expect much more of ourselves than we do of others. The trick is to get the balance right. Look at your friends and check out their personalities. If they are all lovely people with nice personalities and a fun outlook on life, then the chances are you are too. After all, we tend to be friends with people who are mirrors of ourselves. So if they're lovely, you must be too.

As a parting shot, let's just get one thing straight right now - 'beauty is in the eye of the beholder'. Better still, it's someone's personality that makes them beautiful or ugly. Think about it. Good looks can get you part of the way but having a dud personality will get you nowhere! ★

Be
happy!

useful addresses

HELP ORGANISATIONS

ABC (Anti Bullying Campaign)
10 Borough High Street
London SE1 9QQ
Tel no: 0171 378 1446

ADFAM
5th floor, Epworth House,
25 City Road
London EC1Y 1AA
Tel no: 0171 638 3700
(Support for the friends and families of drug users.)

Brook Advisory Centres Central Office
165 Grays Inn Road
London WC1X 8UD
(For all aspects of women's sexual health.)
For details of your nearest Brook Advisory Centre,
phone 0171 708 1234
0171 713 9000

Childline
Tel no: 0800 1111
(Freefone 365 days a year.)

Childwatch
206 Hessle Road
Hull
North Humberside HU3 3BE
Tel no: 0482 25552

CRUSE Bereavement Care
126 Sheen Road
Richmond
Surrey TW9 1UR
For appointments: 0181 940 4818
Helpline: 0181 332 7227

Family Planning Clinics
For details of your nearest Family Planning Clinic,
phone 0171 636 7866

Kidscape
152 Buckingham Palace Road
London SW1W 9TR
Tel no: 0171 730 3300

London Friend
86 Caledonian Road
London N1 9DN
Tel no: 0171 837 3337
(A nationwide agency offering confidential help to anyone
worried about their sexuality.)

MIND
Granta House
15-19 Broadway
Stratford
London E15 4BQ
Tel no: 0181 519 2122
(For information on all aspects of mental health, including
depression.)

NSPCC (the National Society for the Prevention of Cruelty to
Children)
National Centre
42 Curtain Road
London EC2A 3NH
Tel no: 0171 825 2500
24 hour helpline: 0800 800 500

The Bristol Crisis Service for Women
PO Box 654
Bristol BS99 1XH
(This association specialises in helping women who injure
themselves.)

The Eating Disorders Association
Sackville Place
44 Magdalen Street
Norwich
Norfolk NR3 1JE
Tel no: 01603 621 414
(For help with Anorexia Nervosa and Bulimia.)

The Lesbian and Gay Switchboard
BM Switchboard
London WC1N 3XX
Tel no: 0171 837 7324
(24 hour information and help for anyone who is worried about
their sexuality.)

The Samaritans
Tel no: 0171 734 2800
(For confidential counselling.)
For your nearest branch, look in your local phone directory
under 'S'.

The Women's Nationwide Cancer Control Campaign
Suna House
128/130 Curtain Road
London EC2A 3AR
Tel no: 0171 729 1735
(For a leaflet on how to check your breasts.)

Parent's Friend
c/o Voluntary Action Leeds
Stringer House
34 Lupton St.
Hunslet
Leeds LS10 2QW
Tel no: 01132 674 627
(A voluntary organisation run by and for parents with gay sons
or lesbian daughters.)

Rape Crisis Centre
PO Box 69
London WC1X 9NJ
Tel no: 0171 837 1600
(For confidential help with all kinds of sexual abuse.)

Copyright © 1995 Anita Naik

The right of Anita Naik to be identified as the author of the work has been asserted by her in accordance with the Copyright, Designs and Patents Act 1988

Cover artwork by Nick Sharratt

Inside artwork by James Tyrrell

Published by Hodder Children's Books 1995

10 9 8 7 6 5 4 3 2 1

All rights reserved. No part of this publication may be reproduced, stored in a retrieval system, or transmitted, in any form or by any means without the prior written permission of the publisher, nor be otherwise circulated in any form of binding or cover other than that which it is published and without a similar condition being imposed on the Publisher.

ISBN 0 340 634383

Printed by Cox and Wyman

Hodder Children's Books
A division of Hodder Headline plc
338 Euston Road
London NW1 3BH